D1373951

WITHDRAWN

The Data Processing
Manager's Survival Manual

QA
76
.9
M3
S56
1982

The Data Processing Manager's Survival Manual

A Guide for Managing People and Resources

Larry M. Singer

1807 1982

175 YEARS OF PUBLISHING

A Wiley-Interscience Publication

John Wiley & Sons

New York • Chichester • Brisbane • Toronto • Singapore

Copyright © 1982 by John Wiley & Sons, Inc.

All rights reserved. Published simultaneously in Canada.

Reproduction or translation of any part of this work
beyond that permitted by Section 107 or 108 of the
1976 United States Copyright Act without the permission
of the copyright owner is unlawful. Requests for
permission or further information should be addressed to
the Permissions Department, John Wiley & Sons, Inc.

This publication is designed to provide accurate and
authoritative information in regard to the subject
matter covered. It is sold with the understanding that
the publisher is not engaged in rendering legal, accounting,
or other professional service. If legal advice or other
expert assistance is required, the services of a competent
professional person should be sought. *From a Declaration
of Principles jointly adopted by a Committee of the
American Bar Association and a Committee of Publishers.*

Library of Congress Cataloging in Publication Data:

Singer, Larry M. (Larry Martin), 1946-
    The data processing manager's survival manual.

    "A Wiley-Interscience publication."
    Bibliography: p.
    Includes index.
    1. Electronic data processing—Management.
I. Title.

QA76.9.M3S56   1982   001.64'068   82-10836
ISBN 0-471-86476-5

Printed in the United States of America

10   9   8   7   6   5   4   3   2

Preface

Managing a data processing department today is like trying to build the Tower of Babel *after* God made every worker speak a different language. The final objective may be clear, but everyone seems to be going a different way with a unique set of rules. No one seems to be in full control of the applications, hardware, software, or even the people.

The rapidly changing technology of the 1980s and unsettled business conditions have combined to make data processing management an even more complicated job. Critical and expensive business decisions are often made by people who were technicians just a few years ago and are not yet prepared for the high-level management judgments required in the 1980s and beyond. Senior company executives look at the data processing field and shake their heads in frustration because many of those critical decisions are badly made.

If data processing managers are a part of the problem, they are also part of the solution. With proper management direction and effective management philosophies, most DP supervisors, managers, and directors can learn to control the data processing nightmare instead of allowing the nightmare to control them.

This book presents a series of guidelines and procedures which are based upon three fundamental concepts:

1   "Egoless management," in which managers are more concerned with job responsibilities and total performance than their own egos.

2   "Downward management," in which managers are more concerned with the people who report to them than with impressing the boss.

3   "Active management," in which managers actively try to solve and prevent problems instead of hoping they will disappear.

v

The decade of the 1980s is filled with exciting challenges for almost everyone in the data processing world. But for a manager, beyond the glitter of microprocessors, relational data bases, application development systems, and satellite communications, lies the same challenge faced by other managers of the past few thousand years. The challenge is simply to discover the best possible way to manage people and resources to accomplish a goal.

Larry M. Singer

Columbus, Ohio
September 1982

Acknowledgments

The management philosophy for data processing presented in this book developed out of my own observations of managers, managing my own staff, and being managed myself. All the people in my professional life played some part in helping me develop this "egoless management" philosophy.

Portions of two chapters were based on my previously published articles in *Computerworld*: "Attacking Maintenance Costs" (September 8, 1980) and "People—The Forgotten Resource" (January 12, 1981). I thank CW Communications for permission to use that original material.

My wife, Carolyn, deserves special thanks for helping prepare the manuscript.

Finally, I want to thank John Mahaney, my editor, who originally suggested this book.

♂

Contents

1

Data Processing Management: What Is It?

WHO ARE THOSE PEOPLE?

Find a pair of data processing managers having a drink or discussing problems they have with their respective bosses, and you may hear the conversation turn to the question, "Are good, successful managers born or are they made?" Everyone in data processing seems to have his or her own opinion, and many DP professionals cannot even agree upon how to define a successful DP manager. One school of thought maintains that good DP executives do not even need technical data processing training because their primary job responsibility is to efficiently manage those individuals who do have the necessary technical skills. Another theory holds that only experienced technicians can survive as managers because of their responsibility to make expensive and highly complex technical and business decisions which will have a significant impact on the organization. A third belief, usually agreed on after several drinks, is that the job of a DP manager is so impossible that no one in his or her right mind would even want it! This same attitude holds true for those in middle- or junior-level management, although the first-level supervisors often wish they could move up the career ladder to leave their problems behind. The second- and middle-level managers usually know better.

Perhaps there are individuals who are born managers, who have some instinct for effectively handling people, projects, tasks, software, and hardware, and who can manage a $400,000 hardware purchase as easily as they can work out a serious difference of opinion between a data entry clerk and the data entry supervisor. The final hardware selection proves to be the correct choice both financially and technically, and both data entry people leave the manager's office thinking they have worked out their problem themselves. Yes, there are such managers in data processing as there are in many other businesses and professions—rare individuals lucky enough to have the right combination of chromosomes and environment to develop their natural talents.

Unfortunately for the business world, most data processing managers are not that lucky. In many cases they stumble along with vague ideas about management and supervision which they have acquired through trial and error, or from reading a few books on general management theory, or from following the management style of their superiors. Of course, this higher level manager may have learned his or her own management techniques through trial and error, from reading a few books on general management theory, or from following the style of his or her own superior. Rarely in a data processing environment does one find a manager or supervisor who has developed a management style through conscious, planned, and dedicated effort that recognizes his or her management obligation as the primary reason for the position. Rather, the typical DP manager is like a fish out of water or, to put the situation in more technical terms, like a programmer without a coding pad.

This description of data processing management should not be surprising since the business of data processing grew almost as fast as did the technology itself. A company that started with a single programmer writing an order entry system for an IBM 1400 series computer five years later found itself with that same programmer managing 18 people and a large, expensive computer system with very time-critical on-line processing. DP managers were almost always hired as technicians and became managers as the result of seniority, rapid growth of the company, explosive growth of the data processing department, or just plain luck. For a number of years these technicians-turned-managers could handle their jobs and associated problems in a reasonably satisfactory manner. In the 1960s and 1970s, the answer to everything was *technology*, and companies believed—with the support of their very friendly hardware vendors—that most problems and needs could be met by hiring a few more programmers and signing up for the next larger and more powerful CPU. In the late 1970s, for reasons to be explained later in this chapter, that easy, comforting, and remarkably handy practice came to a screeching halt.

In the 1980s, maintaining the status quo will be for most companies, almost an admission of defeat. The rapidly changing computer technology, high turnover in the professional ranks, improving software, and unsettled business conditions have all combined to make the data processing environment more complex and challenging. Yesterday, a hardware choice involved a comparison between an IBM 370/135 and the IBM 370/138. Today, the choice may be among IBM and several excellent plug-compatible vendors, with software capability playing perhaps the dominant role in the decision process. In the early 1970s, a DP manager's hardest personnel problem may have been deciding which of three programmers to hire. In the late 1970s, the hardest personnel problem may have been a 50 percent yearly turnover in staff.

The situation should not be viewed as hopeless, any more than the advent of a new technology such as the data base machine should demoralize current data base users. Making the best of a problem has been a tradition of most DP professionals, and a management crisis should be approached as a problem to be solved. *The means to solve that problem lie in training the DP manager to be a manager first and a technician second.* The complex and frustrating problems faced by any data processing executive—or even a newly appointed project leader—are managerial rather than technical problems. They can be solved or significantly reduced as long as data processing managers regard management as a skill rather than a rare, inborn, and mysterious gift. Programmers are not born knowing COBOL, and managers are not born knowing how to manage. Certain personality characteristics do help make someone a good COBOL programmer, just as certain other personality traits tend to make a good manager a better one, but the key to job success is still training and education. Of course, not everyone can become a COBOL programmer, and not everyone in data processing can become a manager or supervisor.

It does not matter if the manager has 10 years of experience in managing people or only one day; managers at any level can profit from considering techniques and methods to improve their job skills. There is nothing wrong with a COBOL or ASSEMBLER programmer admitting he or she is not the world's greatest programmer and would like some additional training, and there is also nothing unusual about a manager making the same statement. Indeed, the managers, supervisors, or executives who think they are "perfect" and cannot waste their time in self-examination are usually the ones who need management training the most. If they are lucky, senior management will force them to take such training. If they are not so lucky, they will continue to stumble around making the same management mistakes year after year.

The classic definition of a manager as one who works through others does indeed apply to data processing, although it appears that more DP management people tend to get directly involved with technical and procedural matters than corresponding managers in such fields as accounting and engineering. Actually, the data processing environment does make unusual demands upon both staff and management, but the basic definition of a manager still holds true. A supervisor or project leader can function as manager or senior staff person at any given moment, and most first-level supervisors find themselves performing both roles each day. There is nothing intrinsically wrong with a position that combines true management with "hands on" responsibility, as long as the manager understands that supervising people requires different skills, temperament, and "mental set" than functioning as a "doer."

The personality characteristics of a successful manager are both interesting and elusive. Most authorities claim that the best managers and supervisors tend to be levelheaded and possess an even, stable disposition. An excitable and high-strung person is not suited to handling job pressures or touchy interpersonal conflicts which involve other highly excitable people. Such managers develop reputations for causing more problems and can help trigger a high turnover among the staff. Unstable professionals are recognized by frequent outbursts or sarcastic remarks to users and others in the department and should not be promoted to any management position unless they can positively demonstrate control over their behavior in a high-pressure environment.

A second useful personality trait which is frequently overlooked is the ability to listen. Too often, a manager finds himself talking while subordinates merely sit and listen. This practice leads to one-sided communication and the impression that the manager is somehow in direct control over the problems and projects of the section. But any manager who is in a position of authority must not only work through others, as proposed by the classical definition of a manager, but must also receive information through these same people. Supervisors or managers who do not listen to the ideas and suggestions of their staff not only miss valuable information but actually limit their range of options and choices. Although managers have a responsibility to teach and instruct their junior employees, it is no secret that managers can often learn just as much from their staff. Managers who do not listen effectively build walls around themselves that limit their personal, professional, and company growth.

An equally valuable skill is the ability to make decisions based on all available evidence. Data processing by its very nature is a complex area and usually requires decisions based upon proven facts, educated guesses, or outright hunches, and the decision maker needs to separate those categories without allowing emotions and personal feelings to interfere. Also, managers should be able to consider multiple aspects of a problem and make decisions based on the entire situation without being swayed by outstanding particulars. A good project leader, for example, when faced with a rerun decision, can plan the procedure by considering human resources, computer time, relative risks, and business needs. The programming manager planning a new order entry system must be able to develop a realistic project schedule that considers such diverse factors as test-time availability, skill of the project team, and cooperation of the users. In general, the higher the management-level position, the more complex and diverse the factors affecting major decisions and plans. The ultimately complex position might be an MIS director for a large, multinational corporation who must consider such areas as distributed processing, satellite communication, and long-range corporate plans.

The fourth requirement is a concern for people rather than objects or physical actions. Staff members who are "doers" tend to focus on specific assignments, such as programming changes or system designs, whereas managers should show a concern not only for the final results, but for the people behind the programming changes and the system design proposals. A manager who lacks a strong human orientation may appear to be highly successful, and the "key man" of his or her section, but this individual will eventually stagnate because he or she has neglected his or her primary management responsibility. It is important to complete the project design proposal for the accounts payable system, but it is the manager's job to develop the talent necessary to complete a good design and not to complete the design himself. Developing and training a staff can only be done by people-oriented managers who realize that *true management means allowing the staff to be the "heroes."* In fact, one can usually identify managers who are not people-oriented by their image as the only one in the section able to get things done. They may indeed be superstars, but if they retain their crowns at the expense of the employees, they should be quietly relieved of management positions.

Another important skill is the ability to treat people in a fair and evenhanded manner. Even those employees who present an image of the hard-nosed and cynical professional can react negatively when they are not treated on a par with their peers. Although the world does not promise fair and equitable treatment to everyone, most employees still desire some measure of fairness, and mangers who consistently allow personal feelings to interfere with decisions will not be successful.

Supervisors argue that, as a result of their daily interaction with employees, they tend to feel positively toward some and negatively toward others. Any manager or supervisor will develop such preferences, but he or she can still be a fair and responsible manager by separating those feelings from the work environment. Fairness is an absolute necessity—it may never be perfect, but it should be a personal goal for all managers in the data processing department.

A final personality trait that leads to successful management is a positive attitude as opposed to a negative or neutral attitude. Employees often mirror the emotions of their supervisors, and first-level supervisors often copy their attitudes from those of their managers. One high-level management individual with a neutral or uncaring attitude toward the company can spread that unproductive feeling to many others in the organization. Obviously, any normal individual has mood swings, but an experienced and competent manager will try to hide such a mood slump from the employees. Personal or family problems, physical conditions, or work problems can all combine to form a temporary depression and poor attitude. A manager, however, loses the right to show these emotions during the business day.

THE MEASURE OF SUCCESS

Judging a manager's success in any business is difficult, but it may be twice as hard to evaluate a data processing manager or supervisor. One important reason is that the DP environment is in constant flux with the job requirements able to change overnight. A DP executive who is accustomed to disregarding costs and expenditures may suddenly be forced into an immediate program of cost control. A project leader who has supervised maintenance activity on the inventory system for the past two years may be given the job of developing a new order entry system. In both cases, although the essential and basic management skills required are the same, the external and objective measure of success used by the company will be dramatically different. The executive will be judged by how much he or she can shave the monthly expenditures, and the project leader will be rated upon the completeness of the new system design. External measures and ratings are important, but they are not the total picture for any employee who is truly a manager.

In fact, managers and supervisors should be evaluated in two ways: by the objective goals of the department and company defined for them, such as supporting the production general ledger system or designing a new sales reporting application, and by their management skills. It may be argued that managers who do not meet company goals or complete major assignments are unsuccessful, but a closer analysis is required to determine the reasons for their failure to meet those goals. If Kevin, the systems and programming manager, cannot seem to make the promised revisions to the accounts payable system on time, his manager must consider possible deficiencies in Kevin's management ability. Perhaps the entire job situation prevented him from reasonably completing the accounts payable project, or perhaps he lacked the necessary skills to properly motivate his staff. Without certain basic management skills, a manager is severely handicapped, but it is inappropriate to assume a lack of management skills as the reason for not meeting a deadline or completing a project.

Some managers are extremely difficult to judge because they put great effort into developing a public image. They are primarily concerned with their image rather than the accomplishment of external goals or management successes. One can recognize these people by the classic description: They are in charge of everything but responsible for nothing! If the operations manager takes personal credit for an extra effort by the Thursday night shift but does not take responsibility for an error in month-end processing by the Saturday morning production crew, he or she may be excessively concerned with public image and not concerned enough with job responsibilities. This manager may carefully publicize his or her own successes but try to shift the responsiblity for mistakes and missed deadlines onto employees or other departments. Another frequent example is the manager or supervisor who exaggerates the significance of a particular task and makes it appear ten times more complicated and important than it really is. Year-end processing in a bank may indeed be a complex and tricky project, but an effective manager will spend less time complaining about the deadline and more time planning ways to make it less troublesome. Any observer of organizations in action can usually spot the managers, supervisors, and executives who are "political animals" and place their personal image consistently ahead of their employees, department, or even the company which pays their salary.

The opposite type of manager is even harder to evaluate! Supervisors who tend to be quiet, reserved, and not overly aggressive may not publicize their efforts and successes for one of two reasons. First, they simply may not have the need to talk about achievements, or second, they may not have anything worthwhile to brag about. It is the difficult job of the senior manager to discover which reason is applicable in any particular situation. In some cases, managers may not feel the need to present successes to management because they manage "downward" rather than "upward" and believe that their senior manager will eventually realize their worth. This philosophy is justified only if that senior manager has enough sensitive managerial skills to separate the performers from the public relations experts.

Evaluating other managers requires a high degree of what can be called "analytical people skills," or the ability to look at people objectively without personal feelings and with a strong desire to judge their performances based upon actual facts rather than public image. This critical examination should be based upon an understanding of the specific environment, the problems faced by the manager, and a knowledge of what would be expected of a good manager.

RELATIONSHIPS WITH OTHER MANAGERS

Data processing managers typically interact with line managers and employees of other departments. A frequently discussed problem in data processing circles is the complicated interaction between technical managers and managers of other departments. User managers and customers both complain that they have a hard time understanding data processing people and that mutual projects tend to disintegrate into a morass of finger pointing and mutual distrust.

The attitude of managers is the single most important factor in determining the success or failure of the relationship. If each person considers himself partially dependent upon others in the organization, the relationships will tend to be more positive and cooperative. If, on the other hand, each manager believes his or her goal should be to protect a personal empire and expand his or her influence at the expense of others, the relationship will be strained and unproductive for both parties.

Observers of modern corporate and business life report that many data processing professionals at all levels tend to have the attitude that because the data processing environment is so complex the word of the DP department should never be questioned. This obviously leads to a general feeling of superiority which can damage an otherwise productive and satisfactory relationship between managers or professionals. Certainly, a data base design question is complicated and cannot be adequately explained during a coffee break in the company cafeteria, but neither can the logic behind a reorganization of the general ledger chart of accounts, or the legal ramifications behind credit payments in charge account systems, or the principles of the circuitry in the new air conditioner unit just installed by the engineering department. Any reasonable question from a user or other interested person should be answered with enough detail to explain the problem or concept. Although at certain times a question may be purely rhetorical, in other instances that same question may deserve a factual explanation of the technical and business considerations.

Managers should make a special effort to fight the tendency to gloss over questions that at first glance appear impossible to explain. The engineering division director can explain how a voice gets from the transmitter to a receiver unit by giving a four-hour lecture starting with the theory of electromagnetic radiation or by drawing a simple diagram that shows a radio wave travelling between the transmitter antenna and the radio antenna. The systems and programming manager might explain a 45-day estimate for a simple change to the general ledger reporting system by detailing the complex changes required in the file structure or by telling the accounting manager that the modification involves 30 separate modules.

The traditional request to "take my word for it" will not be satisfactory in the 1980s when the accounting manager has a 14-year-old daughter who writes programs on her own microcomputer while eating pizza with one hand and nibbling potato chips with the other.

A successful relationship between managers can also be developed by a willingness to occasionally disregard official procedures and bend the rules. That may sound like heresy, but in the real world of data processing there are often special situations in which following approved procedures is not justified and would cost more time and effort than simply forgetting the rules and getting the job done. "Hard-nosed" DP managers may comfort themselves with the belief that they are acting professionally by always sticking to the book, while in reality they are creating inefficiency and resentment. Of course, any unreasonably strict attitude by data processing personnel will usually be matched by an equally "hard-nosed" response from the user sections, since people tend to remember a lack of cooperation and are anxious to return the favor.

The successful DP manager is willing to consider each situation and adjust procedures and rules. If the accounts payable manager, for example, has a project in progress to add seven new data fields to her aging report and suddenly finds two data elements she had missed during the initial project definition, the programming manager may be within his rights to demand a formal reappraisal of the project, including written, detailed requests from the accounting staff. Or, he may simply ask the programmer to add those two extra fields to the program logic. In this case it may be less costly from the company's viewpoint to allow the programmer to slightly enlarge the project rather than formalize a new request. Besides being more efficient, this minor bending of rules serves as a demonstration of data processing's concern for getting the job done. The rule bending should stop if the modifications would interfere with a mutually accepted deadline. In the final analysis, in any well-run organization, the managers who are wise enough to consider the total organizational viewpoint will usually be the most successful and productive.

The last requirement for a successful DP-user relationship is for the management and staff of the data processing section to understand that information processing is by its very nature a service organization for the users and the user departments. This is true whether the users are cash customers of a time-sharing computer service company or in-house users of the application production systems. If the weekly sales reports are late or incorrect, the expensive data processing section is of little value to the merchandising division. Without payroll reports from the computer, the payroll personnel have no use for the computer or the people who program and operate the machines. Everything done in the data processing installation should either directly or indirectly benefit the other sections of the organization or the customers. A manager who is overly concerned with his or her own importance, the powerful new data base system, or the new on-line transaction processing capability, may forget that the job, the data base system and the on-line processing exist for the sole purpose of filling a business need.

MANAGING UPWARD OR DOWNWARD

Every manager or supervisor interacts not only with customers, users, and colleagues, but also with subordinates and superiors. Everyone has a boss to report to. Observation shows that some managers tend to direct a major part of their attention toward either their subordinates (who may themselves be either managers or staff people) or their own managers. One theory that supports the "upward management" concept is that a manager or staff person will be successful primarily by making the boss happy. Managers who direct their efforts toward their own employees are following the "downward management" approach.

A manager whose primary goal is to satisfy the superiors may become obsessed with real or imagined directives from higher management and allocate people and machine resources toward meeting them. Certainly, it is logical to attempt to satisfy one's superior and make the boss happy, but an overzealous manager who continually manages upward may reduce a section's total effectiveness. One obvious reason is that many comments and suggestions which come from those in authority are not demands or requests, but simply ideas that the manager may want considered. In some situations they are totally inappropriate. In other cases, an offhand remark may be just the right idea to handle a specific situation. It is the job of every manager to evaluate comments and suggestions from superiors with the same care given to suggestions from subordinates. Orders must be followed, but suggestions are not orders. A bad idea is a bad idea, whether it comes from the new programmer trainee or from the director of MIS. A manager will certainly use more tact in telling the MIS director why his or her suggestion is not exactly the best than in telling the new trainee, but the net result should be the same.

Although higher management does set priorities and general policy, it is still the responsibility of a subordinate manager to determine the best way to get there.

The potentially unhealthy emphasis caused by managing upward is demonstrated by a variety of actions and decisions. Such managers have a strong tendency to preserve the status quo and not "rock the boat" with proposed changes, unless, of course, such a proposal comes from their superiors. They will tend to downplay ideas from the staff if they are not obviously part of the current management thinking and will not encourage meaningful questions from employees. Questions and discussion will be allowed, but they will seldom concern the important issues that need to be addressed by both staff and management.

Another unproductive tendency will be a lack of emphasis on staff development. People who think their primary responsibilities lie in pleasing the boss will quite naturally assume that their employees have the same obligation. Staff improvements of technical, professional, or managerial skills are generally not projects launched in order to please a boss—in fact, from a true management perspective, it is just these activities which will pay dividends to the company, the employees, and finally to the employees' managers on a long-range basis. Successful executives must consider both the short-range and long-range benefits in managing their employees. Supervisors or managers who want their people to make them look good will tend to discourage activities that do not contribute to that immediate goal and hence will overlook long-range departmental improvements.

The manager of the opposite extreme will also have trouble performing supervisory duties. If a manager is overly concerned with a particular job, area of responsibility, and staff, he or she may fail to pick up significant cues that can and should come from senior management. These cues will concern company policy as well as departmental or divisional philosophy and goals. Such a manager may take an adversary position with superiors and make decisions partially in defiance of the boss. Obviously, this attitude is unproductive and can demoralize the manager, the staff, and the manager's superior. Employees will soon pick up on the friction and personal conflict and will spend time worrying about personality conflicts rather than productive work.

Which approach, then, is the best for a successful executive? The answer is to consider the primary job responsibility of a manger, which is to successfully manage and control his or her area of application systems, hardware, and people. Concern for personal career goals is admirable, and one should always try to satisfy the boss, but the emphasis should be on managing downward rather than upward. The higher level manager cannot be expected to understand the total picture of the particular section or department and cannot know as much detail as the manager in charge. Indeed, if the higher level manager did know as much as the subordinate manager, there would be no need for that subordinate position! Besides, no management job description will ever state in writing that a manager's primary role is to please the boss. Rather, managers are given executive or supervisory positions with the primary goal of accomplishing a given purpose, and they cannot successfully accomplish that purpose if they spend their time attending to the needs of their superiors. If managers are simply extensions of the boss, they are not true managers, and can probably be replaced by others at far lower cost.

THE ULTIMATE MANAGEMENT QUESTION: WHY?

DP staff professionals firmly believe that supervisors and managers have an internal tape recorder which repeats the question, "How soon will it be done?" at 20-minute intervals from 9:00 A.M. to 5:00 P.M. every working day. That may indeed be a frequent question, but it usually comes from managers who are unsure of their role in the organization. Data processing is action oriented, but far too many managers are concerned only with deadlines and completion dates and fail to let staff personnel assume responsibility for at least some of those important concerns. They see themselves serving as external motivators for employees who may require constant reminders about their work assignments, but they also succeed in irritating those who are capable of handling obligations themselves. In many situations, the professional or clerical staff does not need such external motivation, but the manager provides it anyway. Perhaps he or she fails to understand the self-motivation concept, or underestimates the capabilities of the staff, or simply does not know what else a manager should be doing.

The effective manager can transfer many daily responsibilities of production support or development milestones to the staff, which can include computer operators, data entry operators, programmers, or clerical support personnel. It is amazing how much responsibility people can handle when given the chance. Indeed, a solid program of staff development should allow the manager to retreat somewhat from the daily or even hourly problems and ultimately serve as a resource to his employees.

As a resource, the manager has a responsibility not only to monitor the completion of assigned projects and tasks, but also to constantly ask the question "Why?" Literally everything in a data processing organization that includes technical, procedural, and business aspects needs to be questioned from a managerial view.

Only in the more routine jobs, such as data entry, do employees perform fairly mechanical and straightforward operations. In most other positions an employee makes a continual series of decisions about which job to run next, how to program a particular update logic, and how to design the new on-line inventory system. These daily decisions and judgments are so common that most DP employees do not realize the decision-making nature of their jobs, but such a wide range of choices is intrinsic to data processing. A programmer, for example, can choose what she considers a good way to code a cost calculation routine, but her logic may be impossible for anyone else to decipher and will cost the company thousands of dollars to document, debug, and eventually rewrite. An operator may decide to release production jobs in the traditional first-in first-out manner without trying to balance CPU and peripheral resources. A systems analyst can design an application change but miss an alternate method that would take half the time and reduce machine requirements by a factor of two. Far too many similar choices are made routinely and with little thought regarding consequences. An operator, for example, may not fully realize that his minute-by-minute decisions can actually affect the productivity and efficiency of a multimillion dollar computer system.

Successful managers should question all decisions made by their staff, even if the questioning is never verbalized. Occasionally, the matter at hand is so trivial that it may not be worth the time to talk about, or the employee may be so committed to a chosen course of action as to become defensive if challenged by the manager. But in many situations the manager can offer a question or comment which will make the employee reconsider the coding, system design, or re-run procedure. To borrow a phrase from a popular movie, "Once is not enough," at least in data processing. A second thought, another look at the problem from a different viewpoint, or a simple request to explain a decision can often catch an error or inconsistency caused by a lack of information or bad logic. In other words, the manager or supervisor should act as a filter that allows the best, most productive, and most practical ideas to pass. This is not always possible, but each employee should be prepared with a verbal explanation for his or her decisions. This awareness will often lead to more careful and well-planned work. It is not a matter of sloppiness or lack of concern, but people tend to be slightly more careful if they face a review.

Naturally, it is possible for managers to go overboard and question every action. This is especially irritating if they are not technically qualified to make sound judgments. The manager who asks a systems analyst why he or she has chosen a direct file over an indexed sequential file for the general ledger chart of accounts had better understand the features and drawbacks of each file structure. It is perfectly reasonable, of course, for a nontechnical manager to request a short verbal description of file structures and access methods and the rationale for choosing direct over indexed sequential ones. But a manager who cannot intelligently discuss a topic should not demand explanations he or she cannot comprehend; rather, the manager should ask the staff member enough general questions to at least get a feel for the subject and then ask for an explanation of the decision in question.

A high-level management group, for example, which is examining a recommendation from a techinical project team to purchase a specific data base management system (DBMS), may not understand data base processing but may still demand enough information to allow them to evaluate the recommendation from a business and company viewpoint. The best method is to require a summary of the reasons for and against the recommendation. Such a "good news-bad news" approach is an excellent technique which allows managers to ask the right questions without wasting too much time digging into details that are the responsibility of the staff professional. By demanding to know both sides, or at least verifying that the employee has considered more than one approach, the manager can encourage the staff to develop their own decision making processes. Asking the question "Why?" will not only help get the job done right, but will also become a valuable part of the staff development program. There are at least two sides to every decision, except in data processing, where there are at least 37.

What then, specifically, should managers question? The answer is easy—everything! Obvious targets of these questions are procedures and requirements that have been around for many years. Programmers may have been checking JCL listings and submitting special reporting jobs for the past three years, but isn't there anyone besides a highly paid programmer with ten backed-up work assignments who can check production listings? Could a clerical-level person with proper documentation and training handle the job? Does it need to be done at all? Could a simple one-day project add enough control totals so the system could check itself during production and eliminate the need for manual checking? Does the new application really need to be part of the DBMS, or could it use a conventional file structure and processing method? Does the operations section need to print that 400-page report every day, or could a simple program print the sections requested by users? Does Frank, the accounts payable manager, need that new sort sequence for his special Friday morning summary, or could he use his daily report for the same purpose?

The second aspect of a data processing organization which must be questioned by wise management personnel is the basic structure of the section or department. If the primary language in a shop has always been COBOL, should COBOL be used for the new order entry system, or would one of the new application development languages be faster, easier, and require less maintenance in the future? Should the systems analysts continue to be separated from the programmers, or can they be more productively assigned to the programming supervisor for the duration of a specific project? Does it take a programmer to handle most production support problems, or could several specially trained computer operators successfully perform most of those routine maintenance chores? Does that two-hour backup job have to be run during the busy night shift, or could it be run during the slack time between 5:00 and 7:00 P.M.?

The successful manager of the 1980s will not be afraid to question either the decisions of employees or the policies and procedures of the organization. The questioning must always be done with tact and a genuine concern for people's feelings, but it must be done. The classic excuse, "Well, it's always been done that way before" is no longer satisfactory in data processing.

THE MANAGEMENT ENVIRONMENT

Staff people typically plan their activities around a predetermined set of assignments. Their daily activities may vary tremendously, and in some very busy production support situations, work schedules may be changed every few minutes as a new crisis or request rears its ugly head. But generally, their responsibilities revolve around one or more definite assignments.

Managers, however, function in a multidimensional environment in which their position can change from managing people to being managed. At any given moment a manager might be teaching, supervising, managing, establishing policy, following orders, or giving orders he or she may believe are wrong. Psychologically, such a rapid shifting of roles can cause severe mental strain unless the manager has come to terms with his or her position and responsibilities. The more successful executives try to analyze their own roles and the roles of the people around them, as well as their particular job responsibilities. When their environment changes significantly, they must readjust their roles and redefine their position in the organization.

One characteristic that tends to differentiate between managers and staff personnel is the number of people they interact with on a decision-making level. A clerk in a department store, for example, may deal with several hundred people during a busy day, but he or she will normally follow established rules and procedures and will seldom make a decision that goes against departmental and company policy. A supervisor or manager, on the other hand, may talk with 10 people a day to pass information, handle special situations and problems, make requests, and define rules and procedures.

Managers frequently deal with people and should always try to understand the significant people around them, even if they are not officially part of the organization or section. In fact, some managers have difficulties and problems with their own jobs because they fail to appreciate the people around them who are not their employees but are just as important to their success as a key employee in their own section. The people who can help make or break a manager may not even work for the manager, and this is especially true in data processing.

Contrary to what one might think, the higher up one progresses in a DP department, the greater the number of critical "outside people." A staff member in a nonmanagerial position may depend upon a control clerk to process her job requests, a data entry operator to key her test data, and the programmer in systems software to help her use VSAM files for the first time. The first-level supervisor may depend upon the control clerk and the control section supervisor, the data entry operator, the software programmer, and the systems software manager. The primary reason is that when a staff person has a problem involving cooperation from other units—or a lack of such cooperation—the staff member usually takes the problem to his or her immediate supervisor. Managers typically have a wider choice of people to interact with, although they tend, for the most part, to communicate with other management-level personnel.

Second- and third-level management can depend upon more people for their success than the project leader, if one follows the "downward management" theory which holds that a manager's success depends on the performance of employees, not the satisfaction of his or her superior. A systems and programming manager, for example, will depend on several user section managers and their staff to help resolve problems, answer questions, educate programmers and analysts, and test changes in the application systems. Much of this cooperation is of the "Do me a favor and I'll do you a favor" type, and managers who understand the importance of the people in their environment will make continuing efforts to develop positive relationships. These managers will have a significant head start in the race to achieve success in the data processing world.

There are always occasions, of course, when it is difficult or even impossible to develop a cooperative relationship with a manager or staff member because of personality conflicts, incompatible management philosophies, or outright stubbornness. The software manager may feel that helping application programmers with technical problems is simply not part of his department's professional responsibility, whereas the programming manager believes it is the professional obligation of the software experts to help in difficult situations. The systems and programming manager may then claim it is not her job to help software programmers test application systems under the newest release of the operating system. The shift manager may not like the data entry supervisor and allow this personal antagonism to interfere with the day-by-day interaction between the two, which will then probably lead to disruptions among the employees of the two groups. The programming manager may then blame every other section except her own for mistakes, errors, and delays, which will not only make her unpopular, but may very well cause repercussions which will affect her entire section.

In such circumstances the manager cannot hope to develop a positive relationship but should try to establish a consistently "businesslike" approach to putting the relationship on a purely unemotional basis. The worst response would be to take such a lack of cooperation personally and try to act in the same uncooperative and frustrating manner; adding insult to injury is unproductive for both managers, their sections, and the department as a whole. The correct response requires a well-defined policy created by the unit manager and his staff, in which responsibilities are defined in writing and disputes are documented fairly for higher management to resolve. All meetings and discussions between the two groups should remain calm and professional. If the operations manager is being blamed unfairly for a series of questionable operational decisions, he should make sure the programming manager is aware in writing of the fact that the run instructions were incomplete, or that no one in programming notified the shift supervisor of the special processing for that night. It is easier to negotiate with facts, and in this case the facts must be on paper. In this manner one can attempt to prevent or rectify mistakes so as to reduce the chances of their reoccurrence.

WHAT DO THOSE MANAGERS DO ANYWAY?

Job descriptions for managers are difficult to write, and many practicing data processing management people would answer that question with, "Why, almost everything, of course!" It may seem that their daily job routines vary so much as to make them almost impossible to describe, except in the most vague and general terms. Other managers may never have thought much about what they do. Perhaps they simply follow the example of their predecessors or believe that managers instinctively know what to do. Other managers may perform specific activities because they realize no one else will do them.

Nature may have told the swallows that their primary job responsibility is to fly to Capistrano on a regular schedule, but she forgot to adequately define job duties when she created data processing managers. This oversight can be corrected by analyzing management from a "job performance" viewpoint and evaluating the most common activities performed by practicing DP managers and supervisors—not as specific day-to-day actions but as measurable categories of behavior. If the central thesis of this book is correct and managers can indeed learn to perform their jobs better, it is vital that they know what their jobs are. Doing something better is always smart, but doing the right thing better is even smarter.

Managers spend their time in four general activities: *managing people, planning, making policy,* and *organizing.* Although an executive or manager usually performs other types of assignments, such as consulting with outside departments, most daily activities fall into one of those four categories. It is interesting to analyze how much time a manager spends on each of these activities.

The first and most common managerial activity is *managing people.* This category alone can separate the managers from the non-managers. Managers who do not have people reporting to them may have the title and corresponding salary of a management-level person, but they do not fit the classical definition. Their success and contribution to the company do not depend on having people report to them. Such individuals may be in charge of hardware, machinery, or a very important one-man project—and may be more valuable to the company than the MIS director who has seventy-five people in his or her organization. But this person is not a manager in the traditional sense and does not have to worry about people-management responsibilities.

Any given interaction between an employee and manager can be classified according to the purpose of the verbal interchange. Interestingly, the number and type of verbal interactions will often define a manager's success or failure in terms of people-management skills.

One typical interaction is the *social exchange,* in which manager and employee exchange greetings, talk about the upcoming baseball game, or share a joke about the food in the company cafeteria. A supervisor who spends little time socially interacting with employees will usually rate poorly in people-management skills, except in those very rare situations where the manager is so highly respected that his or her lack of social contact is ignored. The supervisor who has excessive social interaction time will also usually rate poorly. This type of manager will seldom be respected and will appear to be a "pushover" when it comes to employees who like to manage their bosses.

The next interaction is that of *project* or *task management,* when the manager and employee exchange meaningful information regarding a specific work assignment. Psychologically, the employee assumes a subordinate position and attempts to win verbal reward (or at least a lack of verbal disapproval) from the manager. Actually, observation shows that many managers typically respond in a bland, neutral tone, which indicates they are not sure which way to react. The number and type of these "assignment" type interactions are significant; a manager who continually badgers the staff with requests for status reports rapidly becomes "the person to avoid" and will create morale problems that reduce productivity. A supervisor who rarely questions the status of projects and tasks may give the impression that the employees' projects are not important, or the people doing them are not important, or he or she already knows everything. All three effects are demoralizing.

Staff development interaction occurs when the manager and staff member discuss the employee's professional development. The focus is upon the employee as he or she relates to the general departmental or sectional future plans. Career advancement and training are the two most common subjects talked about during these sessions. Supervisors who score poorly in this type of interaction will usually score poorly in general people-management skills, since they are probably "managing upward" and show no obvious concern for their employees' professional growth. Especially in highly technical fields such as data processing, this attitude can be very damaging to the long-range growth of the section, department, and eventually the company.

Other contact between the employee and manager can deal with *evaluation*—rating the performance of the staff member. Every employee needs some feedback on his or her job performance. People differ significantly, however, in the degree of positive reinforcement they need to remain properly motivated, and managers should tailor evaluation interactions separately for each employee. Some staff members will need only occasional feedback from their managers because they have a high degree of internal motivation, whereas others will require almost daily verbal reinforcement to keep them on the right track. Not only must a manager differentiate between the two personality types, but he or she must also be able to modify the level of his verbal evaluations to successfully manage each individual. A supervisor who is not flexible enough to change his or her style will be in serious trouble when faced with an employee who does not precisely fit the manager's theory about verbal reinforcement and evaluation.

Another type of contact is the *general business conversation,* in which the employee and manager discuss the current, past, or future situation in the department or company. Managers who score poorly on general business interaction usually create a communication problem which results in employees complaining that they "never know what's going on." The opposite type of manager will bombard the staff with so much unnecessary information that they cannot concentrate enough upon their work assignments. This type of supervisor is extremely rare.

The most interesting type of interaction in the area of people management is the *brainstorming* session, the potentially most profitable interaction that can occur between an employee and a manager. Both parties attack a problem, design a procedure, or plan a project, on a more or less equal basis. The manager does not dominate the conversation unless he or she has superior knowledge or the employee has little experience with the problem at hand. The manager who encourages brainstorming interaction will greatly stimulate skill development among the staff and will significantly improve morale. Managers who reserve the "thinking" role for themselves may appear to be highly knowledgeable and indispensable to the organization but will produce poorly trained, unmotivated employees. The level of such brainstorming interaction is an excellent clue to the manager's entire philosophy of supervision, and frequent "thinking" sessions will suggest that the manager prefers "downward management," whereas few such interactions will indicate the "upward management" philosophy.

The final category of verbal interaction is the *training session,* in which the employee receives instruction from the supervisor. It is always possible for the employee to take the role of teacher, but it is more common for the employee to assume the role of student. Managers who concentrate on staff development will have higher levels of "training interaction" than managers who do not believe in training.

The second major category of managerial behavior is *planning.* Project leaders and first-line supervisors consider goals that range from a day to a week, or even a month. Rarely do they make longer plans, unless they are responsible for a long-range development or maintenance project. As first-line supervisors train their staffs to be independent and mature, their daily planning role will decrease as the employees assume greater responsibility and manage their own time more efficiently. Any first-line supervisor who is still making daily or even hourly planning decisions is neglecting his or her development duties, or has employees who apparently cannot grow into productive and mature professionals and paraprofessionals. Middle management should examine planning done by first-line managers. Analysts, programmers, operators, and paraprofessionals should be able to plan their hourly and daily work activities without undue dependence upon their immediate supervisors if they have been properly trained and motivated.

Middle- and senior-level executives should plan activities based on a monthly or quarterly cycle and very seldom focus upon weekly or daily problems. It is also their responsibility to review plans made by the first-level supervisors and incorporate them into their own planning goals and objectives. Senior executives should consider time periods of a year or more. They must occasionally become directly involved in the details and crises which arise in any business, especially data processing, but their planning focus should still be long-range rather than short-range.

A frequent and depressing problem in data processing is that managers fail to understand the nature of their own planning responsibilities. As a result, the project leader will plan activities day by day or even hour by hour; the programming manager will look at matters a week or month at a time; and the senior DP management can barely plan beyond the next quarter. No one bothers to prepare for next year, and the department is surprised by a new business requirement, technical advance, or application system requirement. The professional staff never learns to organize and manage their own time for maximum productivity and efficiency. Like any complex organization, a data processing installation can become disorganized, inefficient, and demoralized in the absence of written, sensible, and reasonable plans. Such a department is easily recognizable because the employees never know what they will be working on in the future, since priorities apparently change with the phases of the moon. It takes a strong senior data processing executive to tell the management staff that one reason for this lack of progress is poor or nonexistent planning and that the cure must be administered to all levels in the department.

The time spent planning should be in direct proportion to the level of the manager. First-line supervisors will spend perhaps 10 to 20 percent of their time planning, whereas systems and programming managers will probably spend 30 percent or more in planning. Senior executives may spend more time in planning than in any other single activity.

Making or *interpreting policy* is the third type of activity that most managers spend at least a portion of their time on with senior management occasionally devoting major blocks of their time to formulating rules and procedures.

Organizing is the last category of activity, and it ranks with planning as the responsibility most often ignored. Data processing is extremely vulnerable to rapid external changes which can cause misinformation, misunderstanding, and outright confusion. Procedures can be made virtually obsolete overnight; new developments can require immediate controls, audits, and checks; and the loss of experienced technical talent can shape new requirements. The key to solving many of these problems is organization. People work best when they are organized. Managers who spend significant amounts of time trying to organize and revise procedures, standards, and activities tend to create productive and motivated employees.

MANAGEMENT GOALS: WHAT SHOULD THEY BE?

If a data processing department is truly in a "management crisis," as reflected by low productivity, unresponsive application systems, and a poorly motivated staff, one must evaluate that department as a *business* rather than as a *technology*. The most accurate way to understand the world of data processing is to describe the people and economic forces behind the rapid changes of the past decade—the business angle—especially as it relates to the goals and management philosophy of information systems.

Managing a DP department in the "old days" was easier. Data processing was relatively new in the 1960s and a still largely unknown business in the early 1970s. Both senior management and users quickly found that communication seemed to be the only major problem in dealing with the technical DP people, but with enough trial and error, systems and new applications eventually were accomplished. Especially in the 1960s, everything done by a data processing section was new and exciting, and few people in management thought about how they were doing their jobs.

In the last half of the 1970s, new and disturbing trends developed in the wonderful world of data processing. DP departmental budgets began to explode, and in some growth-oriented companies, they doubled or even tripled in size in one year. Data processing managers having a hard time controlling their $400,000 departments suddenly found themselves working with a million dollar-a-year operation, or even more.

Hardware choices proliferated. At one time, the typical hardware selection was based upon the "It's safer with IBM" philosophy, with several notable exceptions, such as in the banking industry. In the late 1970s, the IBM-compatible hardware vendors came of age and began providing real market competition. Senior DP managers who were accustomed to easy hardware choices soon found themselves with options they were not prepared to handle. At the same time, as software began to be "unbundled," the senior technical staff found new possibilities in terms of hardware-software combinations that had to be considered for every hardware acquisition.

On-line processing became practical and affordable, even for some medium- and small-scale applications. Systems analysts and programmers had to quickly learn new skills, and project managers found themselves responsible for technical procedures that were virtually unknown to them. Data base systems were used in more and more large data applications with varying degrees of success. Cost and time overruns on projects became the rule rather than the exception. Maintenance of existing systems required a minor portion of the total DP dollar in the first few years of the 1970s, but became the largest single programming expense in most shops during the last years of the decade. User departments wanted changes and modification, but DP management always said, "Next year." The DP director lost his or her "hero" badge and soon became the major topic of whispered conversation at quarterly management meetings.

For all these changes (and many more that have not been mentioned), data processing senior-, middle-, and first-level management were simply not prepared. The larger budgets, higher turnover, unsatisfied users, expensive software systems, extensive hardware selection, distributed processing, and the shortage of a trained staff all combined to put the typical manager in a new and confusing position. Some managers even lost their jobs; others migrated to different companies hoping to leave their problems behind; and others tried to ignore the problems with the comforting thought that "Everyone else has the same problems." Still others tried to blame subordinates or specific staff members as the cause of their problems. A few lucky senior executives, however, finally realized that the complex issues of data processing in the late 1970s and the 1980s could be successfully handled by the correct management of hardware, software, and people resources. The only solution was to treat DP problems as management problems.

The questions and concerns that developed during the latter half of the 1970s are now increasing at an exponential rate. Advances in technology are sure to come faster in the 1980s, with such exciting concepts as the data base machine and public data networks. Distributed processing, still in its infancy despite vendor claims to the contrary, promises fundamental changes in data processing from both a technical and business standpoint. At the same time, the 1980s will bring a continual shortage of trained programmers, programmer/ analysts, and systems analysts, to meet ever-increasing demands from users and user groups. The current turnover rate of 10 to 40 percent will probably not improve significantly. What then can DP executives do to solve these problems, make the correct hardware and software choices, meet project deadlines, and still stay within budget?

A large part of the problem can be traced to the fact that too many DP managers still use the same goals they followed when they were technicians. Goals and objectives make up the cornerstones of a management philosophy and will determine a manager's yearly, monthly, daily, and even hourly management-level activities. If he or she is not using the best possible management philosophy, he or she will not be performing a top quality job for the organization and may even prove to be a liability!

The answer is to develop a management philosophy which will help DP managers and their staffs face the problems of the 1980s. Management requirements are changing ever more rapidly in this decade—a DP executive can no longer respond to problems after they erupt in a crisis situation. The old "management by crisis" philosophy simply will be inadequate. Successful DP executives will attack problems and confront issues before they reach the crisis stage. They will worry less about specific project deadlines and fixes to systems and more about strategic issues. Middle- and junior-level management can easily handle the projects, reruns, and fixes without them, but these lower level managers will also learn to modify their behavior to solve management problems as well as technical problems.

Data processing departments and budgets are fast becoming a significant portion of the total company operation. Senior company management in the 1980s will examine the data processing division as an expensive and vital part of the organization and subject them to the same scrutiny as the other divisions. This close examination will also develop because the senior executive staff of the 1980s will be part of the computer age—they will no longer be intimidated by computers when their children use them for homework. Some senior management or the members of the board of directors may have even come from the DP ranks! In the coming decade, company management will ask questions and demand answers for issues that did not exist during the 1970s, and data processing supervisors, managers, and executives must be ready with realistic solutions and positive action plans.

PICK THE RIGHT OBJECTIVES

Line managers in data processing tend to base their goals on specific, individual projects or company objectives. A programming manager may plan to complete the new inventory control system, the functional specifications of the new payroll system, or the long-promised enhancements to the accounts payable package.

Objective goals are important and obviously necessary to any manager, but data processing at this stage of its evolution appears to have made those types of goals and objectives the sole reason for its existence. However, a data processing manager must have a set of management objectives which defines the goals of the data processing organization based on a particular management philosophy. DP directors whose only concern is the development schedule for the new inventory control system are not acting as managers—they are ignoring the complex interaction of hardware, software, and people that they are given to manage.

Data processing itself is not as unique as most DP managers and professionals believe, at least in terms of the "input-processing-output" theory of organization. That is, each functional unit in the organization receives input, processes that information or material in some manner, and produces output. The output may be a new five-ton DC generator for a manufacturing division, or a sales analysis report for the information systems department. Any informations systems division is simply part of an organization or company which has a goal of making a profit or filling a need. Even a data services company which sells computer and software services exists not only for the data processing aspect, but to make a profit for the company. DP managers can best help meet those company goals by managing their own departments in such a way as to solve problems rather than ignore them.

THE FOUR BASIC MANAGEMENT GOALS

The first and foremost goal of DP managers at all levels in the 1980s must be to *stabilize the existing programming, analyst, and operational staff.* Any DP organization with a high rate of turnover—such as 30 percent—cannot function at peak efficiency and will seldom meet its company objectives. Apart from losing valuable people, high turnover causes the rest of the senior staff to be burdened with spending significant amounts of time recruiting and training new staff members. Both company and DP management must understand that high turnover is a costly business loss. In many cases, however, a solution to the turnover problem costs virtually nothing.

The second management goal is to *control costs* in the areas of hardware, software, and people. The days are gone when DP managers are exempt from requirements of cost control. Inflation, high interest rates on borrowed funds, tight market competition, and changing business needs have all combined to force DP managers to prepare themselves for the new requirement to establish an active cost control policy. They must manage large-scale expenditures so as to derive the maximum productivity from the minimum investment. Again, data processing is not unique—this newly matured profession will have to face the same responsibilities as other line departments.

Cost control is more of an attitude than a procedure or method. Some managers tend to think of cost control as slashing hardware costs by canceling the lease on three little-used tape drives or reducing payroll expenses by cutting out an open position. Those techniques are budget reductions and should be viewed as one-time "meat-ax" type measures; they are not in any way part of a true cost control program.

Rather, an effective cost control program in data processing analyzes both the hardware and software in the division for ways to squeeze more results out of the budget. An overloaded CPU on second shift may not be justification for a larger system if third-shift consistently reports unused computer resources. The programming manager who demands two additional headcounts should be able to prove that all current programmers are productive and working on important tasks. Contrary to an obvious belief, money is not the cure for everything.

The third internal management goal of the 1980s must be the principles of *quality control,* an aspect of most business data processing departments that has been sadly lacking. Too often, in the rush to complete critical application systems, the programmers and analysts have cut corners and turned out systems and programs that were not of the highest quality. If programmers in a maintenance environment complain that the production programs are undocumented, hard to follow, and almost impossible to fix, the original problem may have been a lack of concern for quality. In the early days of data processing, the criteria for success was a working, functional program, even if half the logic paths were never tested. Documentation was looked upon as something to fill time when there was nothing important to be done. Efficiency was usually ignored or disregarded as only a minor concern which would not significantly affect the business end of data processing.

Shops with high levels of expensive production maintenance should realize that a lack of standards and quality is often the cause. Also, some high maintenance levels are caused by programmers who did not plan for future changes to existing systems. This indicates either a lack of practical experience or a callous disregard for professional responsibility.

Quality control, incidentally, may be new to data processing, but it is a well-recognized fact of life in most industrial production environments; and the success of the Japanese, and some other industrial nations, is partially due to their concern with quality as well as productivity. Although quality control is different for a department where the output is a computer program rather than a television set, the goals are exactly the same. Is the program easy to read, well-documented, and easy to maintain? If not, the program or system is not a quality job and will eventually cost the company more in maintenance dollars than it took to develop the program in the first place. Although quality takes more time on the front end, the economic justification for quality control procedures is strong. The payoff for a quality job, as opposed to a slipshod job is long-term. DP executives who realize this are well on their way to becoming *true managers rather than simply high-priced project leaders.*

Productivity must also become a management-level goal in the 1980s for everyone in the department, from the senior vice-president in charge of information systems to the newest data entry clerk. Again, the specific project and task goals of the organization require full productivity from each staff member. Tight departmental budgets now require that every programmer, analyst, and manager pull his or her weight and perform to the best of his or her ability. Increasing productivity is a complex issue, but one that must be faced by successful, growth-oriented managers and supervisors. Low productivity that delays projects, evaluations, and final production reports may not be tolerated by companies with definite ideas about the importance of information to their survival.

Management-level goals are extremely hard to measure, and the results may take years to determine. Although turnover in the management ranks is much lower than turnover in the junior staff positions, some managers may not concentrate upon management goals because they do not plan to be around long enough to see the benefits. However, for data processing managers and directors to become part of the corporate management team and to be trusted with company decisions and policy, they must prove their worth. One way is to focus upon the hard-to-measure but vital management-level issues: stability of staff, cost control, quality control, and productivity. Those four objectives should be integrated into the very heart of each manager's personal philosophy.

PRESENTING MANAGEMENT GOALS

Policy documents provide a simple but effective way to inform both senior management and the internal DP staff of the new concerns of data processing management. Such memos or letters need not have a tone that shows criticism or blame of the current or even the preceding staff; rather their wording should show that senior DP management is willing to face the same critical issues that appear every week and month in the trade newspapers and magazines.

Any policy memo or letter will be greeted with an immediate question of "But how?" It is important to stress that no one individual has the answer, but progress will require a team approach. Although management certainly needs to follow up with specific actions and programs, such problems are long-range projects which will have both successes and failures. The letter should be followed up by a general meeting to explain the circumstances and nature of the difficulties as they relate to the individual company.

REORGANIZATION MAY BE THE ANSWER

Any goal, whether it is a long-range management goal or a specific project-level objective, requires tools and techniques. Although an excellent source of those tools is the data processing staff, there are some generalized techniques that can help meet the four basic management-level goals. Although they will seldom, if ever, solve the entire problem, these techniqes can help move the organization toward better and more efficient performance by actively attacking those issues on a positive, honest basis. One technique is to examine the organization of the entire DP department.

The traditional joke in data processing circles is that when all else fails, the manager should reorganize the staff. That tongue-in-cheek advice may be more sound than most professionals realize. An organizational chart developed 10 years ago when data processing was new may not work successfully in the 1980s and may actually contribute to low productivity and high turnover. Or, even if the organization appears to work, some other structure may be more effective. A good data processing management team needs to examine the internal organization regularly and determine if the time is ripe for changes in structure. Although any reorganization will cause temporary problems in staff assignments and some unhappy people, the final results may be well worth the price.

The traditional business data processing installation uses one of two classical organizations for the systems and programming staff: the so-called "system team," in which the staff shares development and maintenance assignments, or the "project team" approach, in which the staff is organized for a specific purpose, such as developing a new payroll system or supporting the current inventory systems.

More and more companies are discovering that the project team approach has distinct advantages over the system team type of organization. One unrecognized reason is that maintenance and production support functions require a vastly different "mental set" than system and program development. When members share responsibilities for maintenance and development, not only is it virtually impossible to plan accurately, but also, both functions usually suffer in terms of quality, morale, and productivity. Although the project team structure introduces other problems, it has certain advantages.

First, maintenance teams of existing application systems can be organized not only to support and update production systems, but also to improve them operationally. Most programmers and analysts take a dim view of merely supporting a system someone else has designed and written and will respond more favorably if they realize their job responsibility includes improving the system. This change alone can improve staff morale and give unmotivated professionals a valid, fulfilling challenge.

Too often in the typical business data processing installation the maintenance function is considered a necessary and unpopular evil. Professionals and their managers try to work themselves out of this responsibility and into something that appears more satisfying. In actuality, production support of existing application systems is usually exasperating, frustrating, complicated, tricky, puzzling, and filled with pressure—precisely the challenge many data processing people like! By according maintenance its rightful position as a specialty in DP, management can often stimulate the staff's creative juices and eventually achieve a significant reduction in costs.

Second, project teams with little or no maintenance responsibility can devote full attention to the specific development project, which makes quality control of that project easier. Planning can be done on a more realistic basis, and one can eliminate major surprises.

Third, setting up a new project team allows members to exchange job responsibilities and project leadership roles. DP management then has a chance to evaluate other senior professionals as potential managers. The common complaint in some shops that few management or supervisor openings exist will be reduced—many other professionals will see at least a chance to have a taste of supervision and project management.

Another possible organizational structure is the "pool" concept, in which programmers, programmer/analysts, and systems analysts are assigned to a professional pool under the direction of a second-level programming and systems manager. Individuals are then assigned to various project leaders and may even become project leaders themselves for specific assignments and tasks. Administratively, the staff still reports to the manager but works under the direction of the assigned project leader. This method insures that professionals have contact with middle management through the systems and programming manager but function as part of a project team. The pool system allows senior management to more effectively control the allocation of programming and system talent, which is often a serious problem in the project of systems team approach. The recent emphasis on "zero based budgeting" is related somewhat to the pool allocation concept in that professional resources must be justified before they are allocated.

In a department with systems teams, the four members of the sales reporting group, for example, would be permanently attached to all production support and development projects that concern sales analysis and sales reporting and, theoretically, would become knowledgeable and proficient in those particular applications. The reality of the situation often does not achieve its apparent logic. Far too often a section is overloaded with work one month and bored the next month, especially if it combines maintenance and development. Project leaders may then dream up tasks and assignments that seem unjustified to second- or even third-level management. Even though the typical project leader will try to fill a void with work assignments, any task requiring more than a few hours work should be *justified*, and the professional pool concept forces first- and second-level managers to look at their resources from a managerial rather than a personal viewpoint.

DP executives tend to be conservative and hesitant about changes in their internal organization. Any change, however, can be made less disruptive if senior DP management considers the reorganization as a move toward better performance, rather than an absolute, final answer to all real or imagined problems. In management terms, any reorganization or restructuring is almost an experiment in managing and organizing human resources.

THE LOYALTY QUESTION

Any management philosophy of the 1980s must address the issue that has divided data processing from the rest of the technological disciplines—the loyalty factor. Senior corporate mangement feels—with valid reason—that DP professionals owe most of their loyalty to themselves and not to the company that pays their salary. The high turnover rate in most data processing installations is only one example.

No one seriously doubts that such an attitude exists: No one even pretends to understand all the complex sociological and psychological reasons for this behavior, but it is not necessary to understand the causes of a problem before attempting to rectify it. Rather, the task is to recognize the problem for what it is—not a purely data processing problem but a management and human problem that can be approached with corrective, positive management action. Some specific techniques to help solve this provlem are:

1   Make sure that all DP employees feel a part of the organization rather than just a member of the data processing department.
Loyalty is impossible unless the professional staff knows what to feel loyal to! One method is to hold regular departmental meetings or training sessions to allow briefings by non-DP managers or company executives. In a manufacturing company, for example, the sales and marketing manager might discuss a product still in the planning stages, or a new area being opened up for future sales. The merchandising executive of a retail or distribution company could describe expansion plans for new stores or present basic information about the merchandising function.

This effort will be harder with the data processing departments than with other parts of the company, usually because data processing people have a habit of considering themselves self-contained entities and not a true part of the total company or corporation. The world of data processing tends to revolve around the computer, not around the company. In the 1980s this attitude must change, starting at the top of the DP executive ladder and working down through the entire chain of command.

2 Use both external and internal resources to show the data processing staff that their efforts and production are important to others in the company.

Too often, in many organizations, the technical staff considers the general ledger report as a mysterious part of the financial system, rather than one of the most important legal and functional reports in the company. They may never have seen the actual report or know how the operating and financial divisions use general ledger reports. In some companies the programmers and analysts who support the financial systems have never even seen the accounting section!

Unfortunately, senior information systems management is usually the only group in the data processing organization that recognizes the importance of the information processing team. Professionals at all levels of the organization, from senior analysts to data entry operators, must have this same understanding—it will eventually help them feel some loyalty and responsibility to their companies. This educational program must be tailored to the individual situation and should continue as a year-round, never-ending project.

3 Provide for more interaction between the technical staff and the user departments.

Traditionally, the senior staff and management have reserved themselves the right of significant user contact, in both new application system design and in production support of current systems. User contact has been looked upon as a "privilege" reserved only for those with long years of service, or for those in management-level positions. In actual practice, this philosophy has caused two serious and degrading problems in most organizations. First, the staff member who is deliberately excluded from user contact meetings feels less a part of the company and may even take this situation as a personal insult. Second, in many cases the first- and second-level managers who have had original contact become "errand boys" trying to relay information between users and the technical staff, which needs firsthand, accurate, and current information.

A more productive management style is to encourage some degree of interchange between the technical staff and selected users. This encouragement will allow the successful DP manager to help solve both the loyalty question and the nagging productivity problems that are caused by a lack of communication between the user groups and the programming staff.

SUMMARY

The technological and human issues of data processing in the 1980s are extremely complex, and there are no easy, simple answers for every organization. However, by applying a sound management philosophy and developing an active, positive management strategy based on those principles, the DP manager of the 1980s can be successful. The key to success, however, is the underlying management philosophy, and this book proposes specific techniques and procedures to solve problems based upon two fundamental concepts.

First, DP managers should practice "egoless management," a style and tradition of managing people that allows supervisors to concentrate upon their jobs rather than upon their position in the company. *The greatest enemy of a manager may be his or her own ego!*

Second, DP managers should "manage downward," as opposed to "managing upward." "Downward" managers are free to concentrate upon their people, assignments, and projects, whereas "upward" managers are usually so occupied with making themselves look good that they are severely handicapped as managers.

With both these concepts and a supporting management structure, the DP manager can meet the challenges of the next decade.

2

Productivity in the 1980s

How to increase productivity in the data processing profession may turn out to be the question of the decade. Information systems management is now faced with high system maintenance costs, high personnel turnover, expensive new technical capabilities, and a shortage of experienced programmer/analysts and systems analysts. User departments are increasing their demand for new systems and applications, while missed project deadlines are becoming a fact of life for DP departments. Distributed processing is opening up a whole new applications concept that will require technicians to think like business people while acting as programmers. The logical solution to these problems is to increase the productivity of the current DP staff.

But how? You can't have the staff start work at 6:00 A.M. rather than 8:00 A.M. on a permanent basis. You can't speed up the assembly line. You also can't stand over them with a whip and chair and tell them to work faster. Is there anything that can be done to increase the daily productivity of programmers, programmer/analysts, and system analysts?

The answer is yes, but some solutions to the productivity problem are difficult and may even require a reevaluation of the typical data processing organization and structure. These actions require either new budget expenditures or a readjustment of the current DP budget, both of which may be hard to justify to company management. Others may appear to be so simple and obvious that some managers may doubt their effectiveness. There are answers, but they are seldom easy.

There is no single solution to the productivity problem, but rather, one can assume a generalized "shotgun" approach, which will attack several problem areas on a broad front. Each data processing department has its own particular characteristics, which either reduce or encourage productivity, and DP management can use the techniques offered in this chapter to mold an individualized program.

Results will usually come slowly, but they will indeed come if management is willing and able to understand the changing needs and environment of data processing in the 1980s.

DP NEEDS PARAPROFESSIONALS

Technology in the 1980s may be advanced by microcomputers, data communication, and data base, but the "business" aspect of information systems can be advanced during this decade by the development of the paraprofessional. In DP shops ranging from the very small to very large, the programmers, analysts, and managers are continually performing clerical and operational tasks which are in no way related to the programming or managerial profession. Rather, these tasks have been assigned to the professional staff because the traditional DP organization consists only of managers, programmers, operators, and data entry operators. Except for positions such as data control clerks, all functions not specifically part of management and operations have usually been left to the programming staff.

The reasons are largely historical. As computerized business systems grew in size and complexity, so did the programmer's responsibility in terms of both production support and job management.

Most production systems, especially business-oriented applications, require clerical and operational support to keep running. A programmer's job became more technically complex as operating systems and features became more powerful, but the original, unofficial job description still included the duties of clerical keypuncher and part-time computer operator. The data processing profession quickly developed a hierarchy of programming titles and jobs which still included many clerical and operational tasks. If a new programmer or analyst questioned these duties, he or she was usually told, "It's just part of the job," or "There is no one else around to do it."

Another reason for the situation is that as technicians were promoted to managerial positions they carried with them attitudes and opinions which may have been valid 10 years ago but are now obsolete. One such attitude is that almost all tasks in a data processing environment require experienced technicians who have a college degree or other technical training. This belief is not only false, but also drastically lowers the productivity of the professional staff by having it perform tasks easily accomplished by less-qualified and lower-paid personnel. Programmers are not necessary for many of the tasks routinely assigned to them, and managers who firmly believe that their organization should consist only of professionals are wasting valuable resources by underestimating the ability of people in clerical positions. Once managers examine their departments from a "managerial" rather than a "technical" standpoint, they will quickly realize that using paraprofessionals can boost productivity.

One very common and disturbing loss of productive programmer and analyst time can occur at the interface with the operations section. In some shops, programmers are almost required to run their own tests and compiles, pick up their listings from the printer, and manually set up special production runs or reruns. The number of labor hours spent in this practice may not be great during a specific week, but the number of interruptions, and their cumulative effect, may be serious. Management should analyze the actual time spent by the programming staff in operational support duties. Such work may need to be done, but who should do it?

Most large- or even medium-sized shops which have excessive programmer involvement can use a full-time "operational support specialist" who is a former computer operator and who can relate well to programmers and their activities. Duties can include running tests, providing rapid and dependable courier service between programming and operations, submitting routine production support jobs, and serving as an interface to the operations section. This individual could also help evaluate and write operational documentation and solve many production problems, formerly requiring help from the programming section. With some JCL training and basic systems knowledge, he or she also could handle some production reruns and restarts and free programmers for other assignments.

A second type of unnecessary programmer activity is excessive user contact. Many programmers want and enjoy customer contact regarding system development, but not many programmers or analysts feel very positive about continual interruptions from users who ask basic production support questions. Examples of frequently asked questions are: "What tran code do I use?" and "How is this field calculated in this report?" and the ever popular "Can you call operations and rush my report?"

Whereas good user documentation will go a long way toward reducing the unnecessary questions, turnover and changes in user departments will always provoke questions from user groups. The traditional solution (or nonsolution) is to have the user ask the programmers, since they are most familiar with the production systems. This procedure does solve the immediate problem for the user manager, but it is the DP or programming section that pays the price in terms of lost productivity. Application system users need support, but programmers are not always the best ones to provide that assistance.

A paraprofessional who is a "systems support specialist" could learn the application systems, study the available user documentation, and serve as the primary interface between user groups and the programming staff. This could be a college graduate or a bright, experienced, clerical-level person who is familiar with the application system input and output. This person should have basic writing skills so he or she could help with creating and maintaining user documentation. With enough application system knowledge, this paraprofessional could help resolve or at least define problems and questions that invariably arise from users.

Probably the most common type of wasted programmer time is

devoted to clerical activities. Most programmers and system analysts spend too many hours filing listings, checking JCL, key entering program changes and test data, writing memos, creating documentation, and performing assorted other duties. DP managers who see a programmer sitting at a typewriter or entering a large set of test data into a CRT terminal should realize the high cost of such clerical work. Programmers and analysts themselves are a good source of information regarding how much of their workday is spent in clerical activities.

A paraprofessional, such as a clerical support specialist with typing or data entry skills, can perform many of the clerical tasks that programmers must do themselves. This requires both DP management and the professional staff to understand that some tasks and activities commonly done by programmers are best done by nonprofessionals. In some departments, the right clerical support person can relieve both managers and the professional staff of many responsibilities and free them for more productive work. The number and nature of daily tasks that can be done by a clerical support person is limited only by the innate capability of the clerical person and the creativity of the management involved.

A general guideline is that one paraprofessional support person is justified for every six to eight programmers and analysts, with the paraprofessional also devoting some time to assisting the manager. The specific type of paraprofessional—operational support specialist, system support specialist, or clerical support specialist—depends on the needs of the individual data processing section. In some cases, a "programming assistant" position may combine two or even three of the support specialist roles. From a productivity standpoint, one support position is usually worth more than one new programming or analyst position, since the productivity of the entire staff can be raised significantly as the number of interruptions to the staff decreases and the morale of the professional staff increases.

EXAMINE WORKING CONDITIONS

Unsatisfactory working conditions can reduce the productivity of both the clerical and professional groups by reducing morale and making it more difficult to work. Before rejecting the idea of improving working conditions as being "too expensive," management must examine the existing loss of productivity in actual dollars.

The most frequent physical problem in DP organizations is the "bullpen" or "common" area where programmers and analysts are located together. Programmers in such an environment report excessive noise and distraction, making it difficult to concentrate and complete their assigned work. Ideally, professionals should have their own office or cubicle, where they have privacy and are free from the distractions of others. An alternative to the common area is to build partitions around each desk. If the budget permits, the DP manager would be wise to call in an office decorating firm that has experience with the newer concepts in office design and can propose a modern, flexible, efficient arrangement of partitions.

Another commonly reported problem is the appearance of offices— it is hard to feel motivated when sitting in a dull, drab room with pipes hanging from the ceiling or walls that obviously need painting. If money is a problem, it may be possible for the company to buy paint and ask the professional staff to volunteer to have a "painting party," with food and refreshments furnished by the company. If the project is approached in a positive manner, it should receive enthusiastic support from those who complain about the drab offices and depressing environment.

A shortage of office supplies or difficulty in obtaining them in a reasonable amount of time is another problem that can reduce productivity because of frustration and resentment. A professional who has legitimate complaints about such basic matters as office supplies or furniture may not be fully motivated to handle job assignments properly.

TOOLS OF THE TRADE

Both programmers and analysts need access to program listings, user documentation, technical manuals, procedure manuals, and many other pieces of information which are the tools of the profession. Programmers, especially, are sensitive to information needs and can waste many unproductive hours searching for facts that can and should be readily available.

Providing these tools is more a matter of ingenuity than money. Program listings should be centrally located and stored in individual folders, rather than binders, which make them hard to get at and impossible to maintain. Modules need indexes so they can be referenced. Technical manuals can be photocopied at a lower cost than that of ordering them from the hardware or software vendor if this is permitted by the individual hardware or software agreements. User documentation should be distributed to the system analysts and programmers for reference. A technical and applications systems library should be set up and maintained so that the professional staff can have access to all available documentation. The goal should be to increase productivity by examining the needs of the particular DP section and trying to solve those needs by saving both steps and time. Efficiency in day-to-day work can then lead to increased productivity.

HIRE OUTSIDE PROFESSIONALS

In some cases, a DP department can stretch its budget and improve total productivity by hiring contract programmers instead of creating additional programmer or analyst positions. This is especially true for projects that are ready for detailed system design or programming, and in situations for which the company does not have sufficient technical resources in a new area, such as establishing a communications network or designing a data base.

Some DP managers have a bias against hiring outside professionals because they would rather use the money for a new full-time position. DP management should compare the true cost of a staff position against hiring contract programmers. Every staff member requires benefits, supervision from others, training from peers, and administrative support. For certain projects, it may be far more efficient and less costly to hire an outside firm at a fixed price or hourly rate. The decision must be based upon facts, not opinions.

Contract DP firms and free-lance programmers range in quality as do programmers—from poor to excellent. Once an outside firm has worked successfully for a DP department, it can become a valuable resource. The contract programmers who do not perform satisfactorily do not have to be hired a second time—this is far easier than firing an employee who is not doing a good job. Although professional consulting companies frown on the practice (and in some cases write a clause in the contract preventing it), some companies are so pleased with contract programmers and analysts that they offer them full-time positions. Two major advantages are that management knows the capabilities of that individual, and the new staff member would be at least partially tained.

THE CURSE OF PAPERWORK

Excessive paperwork is not only a constant complaint of business in this country, but it can also reduce individual productivity by taking up valuable professional time. The nature of our civilization seems to require forms, reports, and memos to serve a multitude of purposes, and data processing as a profession seems particularly liable to mounds of unnecessary or duplicate paperwork.

If the staff or management complains about the time they must spend on the reporting function, it is time to review all required paperwork and eliminate those forms and procedures that are not vital to the organization.

The increase in productivity can be seen almost immediately, since the time formerly spent on paperwork can be devoted to productive projects and tasks. Especially in the larger, more complex data processing installations, reducing paperwork requirements can lead to a more streamlined and efficient operation. Paperwork, after all, must be written by one person, passed to another person, and disposed of by being read, eventually filed, or thrown away. Even redesigning a form for easier use will help reduce the time spent on selective paperwork that cannot be eliminated. All reporting prodecures, including the so-called "status meeting," should be evaluated from a business and control standpoint, and they should be eliminated if they are not justified.

MANAGEMENT DIRECTION

Increasing productivity in data processing is not only a matter of arranging the work environment for maximum efficiency, but also of directing the daily, weekly, monthly, and yearly activities of a department so that people produce more by working "smarter and better." This concept is not to be confused with the classical advice to "plan better," whatever that means. Rather, the idea is to develop a style of short- and long-term management that makes productivity a departmental goal. This style should be manifested in the long-range plans and goals of a department, as well as the daily decisions made by the senior-, middle-, and first-line managers. The following sections discuss specific management policies which will encourage and increase the productivity of any data processing section or installation.

PROJECT AND TASK PLANNING

Much has been written about the need for careful and detailed planning before commencing any major project in data processing, and many shops try to follow well-documented planning procedures for any long-term activity. However, it is just as important to have detailed and careful planning for the smaller, one-person tasks that abound in data processing. Productivity can jump significantly by applying planning techniques to even the most common one-day or one-week tasks.

For example, designing a change to add a new field to a payroll system may involve studying six programs. The analyst, if she has not planned her work before actually starting, may very well retrieve one program at a time from the library and design each change with little regard to the other programs that need changing. But if she has carefully planned the task before starting, she will retrieve all six programs at one time and design the changes from a system standpoint rather than from a program-by-program approach.

Even some experienced data processing professionals who have been around for many years still tend to attack a project or task as though they were assaulting a beachhead with the Marines—brute force may look impressive and will usually get the job done, but that approach rates a zero when it comes to productivity. The solutions for critical production problems or meeting deadlines are generally not found via the famous "Mongolian horde" technique, in which the staff is suddenly doubled or tripled. Many times a manager will find that productivity actually drops as hordes of eager programmers and analysts jump to the rescue with pencils in one hand and hexadecimal calculators in the other. Even without proper direction, planning, and training, the horde may eventually capture the fortified city, but it may very well burn it down in the process.

DP professional staff members should be taught to plan their work so they can accomplish the most in the least amount of time, and this concept requires that the first-line supervisors encourage their staff to plan all tasks on paper, not in their heads. Planning even the simplest tasks and daily activities can significantly increase the productivity of most programmers and analysts. The professional staff must understand that time is valuable and planning is one way to utilize it more efficiently. The first and most frequently overlooked step in successful daily time management is to plan for every task in the day's schedule.

As with major project planning, task planning must have measurable goals. The first-line supervisor should reject plans that follow the simple "code, compile, and test" ritual. Planning requirements should be tempered with common sense. It is not sensible to require a programmer to write a detailed plan which will take longer than the assigned task! With perseverance, however, DP professionals can be taught and encouraged to use planning as an aid to their professional growth.

First-line managers, such as project leaders or shift supervisors, often find it difficult to create a daily plan for themselves because the demands on their time are constantly changing. A production problem in the sales reporting area may suddenly require several managers and professionals. The new programmer trainee may casually mention that he has never used the indexed files which are prevalent in the new shop—a point missed during the initial interview. A request from the Management Information Systems director to explain the delay in the data base produce load will demand action from the managers and professionals involved in that activity. When the only programmer in the section who knows ASSEMBLER takes her two-week trip to Las Vegas, the project leader who wrote two ASSEMBLER programs six years ago may be drafted to fix the abend on the payroll system. Unplanned interruptions can and will occur in every business data processing installation in the world, but first-level managers who build a daily activity schedule around an expectation of constant interruptions are eventually cheating themselves and their position. By planning daily activities, managers will not only set a good example, but will also shape their management thinking into a more productive mode. It is difficult, but it can be done.

For example, at the end of a working day a project leader or second-level manager can list on paper his or her goals for the next working day, such as following up on a production problem, consulting with a systems analyst, or helping to solve that strange communications network abend. Although some days will not follow any prearranged schedule, having a written plan will improve time management when the manager has blocks of time available and can systematically accomplish his or her objectives. A manager—or any employee for that matter—cannot be productive when he or she arrives in the morning and is not immediately ready for work, or at least knows what has to be done. An unplanned day is usually an unproductive one because the employee has not logically arranged his work schedule to accomplish the most in a given amount of time.

SUPERVISE FOR PRODUCTIVITY

The attitude of management toward programmers and analysts can affect the productivity of the staff, since workers tend to follow the style and actions of their immediate supervisors. Project leaders are in an excellent position to develop supervisory techniques to encourage productivity. These techniques are not merely a "push" for the employees to produce more, but a style that encourages success and pride in meeting deadlines.

An obvious but often overlooked method to increase the productivity of the staff is to publicly recognize tasks and projects that are completed, even if they are not done on time. The trick is to reward the successful completion of a project as an event that deserves public notice, although the manager should not praise a project that was delayed due to a lack of effort. If the professional tried—even unsuccessfully—he or she should be recognized in a meeting of peers. The idea is to emphasize that accomplishment will catch the attention of management.

Having weekly sessions with each employee will not only help develop a more positive relationship between the employee and the supervisor, but will also encourage productivity by giving the employee "stand alone" time with his or her manager. These private talks should cover all aspects of pending projects, tasks, and assignments and can help resolve both actual and potential problems discovered through planning. Too often in many business data processing installations, employees feel alienated from the manager and confused about procedures, goals, and problems. Although in many DP shops the members of a project team may interact on an hour-by-hour basis, there is still no substitute for individual and private sessions between staff member and supervisor. Employees differ in their need to have such contact, but even the most experienced and self-motivated professional must have at least one such meeting a month. Junior staff members should have at least one meeting a week. Any manager who fails to recognize this variable need risks confusion, misunderstandings, and a possible ensuing loss of productivity.

The third supervisory technique to increase productivity is to encourage intra-group communication. Professionals in data processing often lose track of the plans and activities of a programming or systems section and become lost in their own responsibilities. Although a few employees will flourish in an isolated atmosphere, most people who need to feel part of a group will develop morale problems and become frustrated. They do not feel a part of a plan or "movement" but rather an isolated pawn in a world that is passing them by. Such attitudes are difficult to verbalize, but a manager who investigates vague feelings of dissatisfaction may discover that the cause of such discontent is a feeling of isolation.

Poor communication among members of a group can lead to complications when several people are trying to work on the same module or change the same applications system. A second-level DP manager who finds that two programmers in one area have been working at cross purposes for several weeks can blame the project leader for two distinct errors: not catching the problem himself, and, not encouraging proper communication among the staff so the programmers themselves could have caught the management error. The time spent in group communication is quickly repaid by the increase in morale, coordination, and the subsequent rise in productivity. After all, the work accomplished in data processing is not strictly a function of time, but rather an integration of both the quantity and quality, and productivity can be increased by upgrading the quality of effort.

The fourth supervisory attitude that can encourage productivity is to promote a team approach if the project leader has enough management skill to pick the right situations and weigh the labor costs against the benefits. If programmers and analysts are encouraged to share ideas, information, and resources by occasionally making a one-person project a joint effort, they will learn each other's strengths and weaknesses and, one hopes, reduce the unproductive time spent on problems previously solved by another programmer. With proper guidance from the manager, these two professionals can make a joint task into a mutually beneficial learning situation.

Joint teamwork will also encourage a feeling of mutual responsibility for all projects in a section. For example, if a programmer must pick up his own listings from the machine room, he should feel some obligation to pick up printouts for his fellow team members which will increase total productivity of the department. If a programmer needs help in using direct access files in COBOL for the first time, she should feel free to ask another programmer for assistance, and that programmer should feel an obligation to help his department by sharing his knowledge. Total departmental productivity should be a concern of the staff as well as management.

Encouraging a professional attitude can often boost productivity by helping the programming, systems, and operational staff realize the importance of their work to the company. Obviously, a lax, uncaring, or even neutral attitude among the professional staff is not conducive to productivity. First-level managers can help create a professional feeling and atmosphere by treating employees with respect, disseminating needed information, insisting that other managers treat their people with courtesy, requiring that the behavior and actions of the staff reflect their importance, and generally setting the best example. Radios in every room, for example, not only are distracting but will also encourage a party atmosphere. Although it is easy to go past the limits of reasonableness and try to foster a rigid and tense departmental atmosphere, most first-level supervisors should have enough basic management skill to create a professional atmosphere and still retain informality and pleasantness.

Another technique which will help supervisors encourage productivity is to teach data processing staff members the art of "multitasking." In most environments a programmer or analyst will be working on a project or assignment that has many subtasks, some of which are dependent on a previous task and others which can be done at any time. A Pert or other project planning chart is an excellent way to display specific tasks that need not be done in a particular phase or sequence, but can be scheduled at almost any free moment during the assignment. Since the majority of data processing projects are "resource dependent" and are restricted by factors such as computer time and user cooperation, the professional will usually meet stopping points during which he is waiting for something. The supervisor can step in at this point and show the staff member tasks that can be done slightly out of logical sequence. Building test JCL, for example, does not have to wait until all programs are linked and ready for testing—it can be done while the programmer is sitting there complaining about turnaround time for the first compile.

The key to successful "multi-tasking" is a well-planned, and carefully detailed set of project requirements. The Hollywood movie producer uses a very well-defined shooting schedule to arrange production in the most efficient manner and films all scenes for one location at the same time. It may not be logical for the actors, but it gets the job done in the most cost-effective manner. The director of *Gone with the Wind* did not burn down Atlanta, put the fire out to film a close-up of Scarlet and Rhett, and then burn down Atlanta a second time! Teaching professionals to identify tasks which can be successfully done out of sequence is an excellent way to keep people busy with productive work and keep them away from idleness. Complaining about test or turnaround time may be a God-given right of every programmer, but it is the responsibility of management to teach that individual how to productively use his or her time when he is through complaining.

A final supervisory attitude that will help increase productivity is a firm policy not to "reinvent the wheel." A coding technique, a file layout, or a project planning method that has already been used and accepted should not be redone. Managers frequently must stress this policy to those professionals who have a disturbing tendency to try new and unproven techniques just for their own satisfaction. Too often, programmers or analysts will ignore previous work experience in the department and create their own technical world, which may actually be a step backward in terms of standardization or productivity. This warning also applies to high-level management decisions involving software or hardware modifications and system designs. Decisions that sound good in theory may later be cursed by those who must maintain the theory when it is finally put into production. The "Keep it simple, stupid!" philosophy is one of the best management axioms ever developed.

DOCUMENTATION IS NOT A MYTH

Most DP executives agree that good documentation will save time and effort in both system development projects and production support situations, but they will still assign documentation efforts such a low priority that documentation never gets off the ground. Part of this reluctance comes from confusion about documentation in general. After all, a documentation project requires written standards, procedures for updating, and a programmer/analyst willing to write the documentation—all three of which are virtually impossible to find at the same time! No wonder documentation is always recommended but seldom implemented. Only in the larger installations can one find full-time documentation specialists who have both technical and writing skills, although many medium-sized companies would be smart to evaluate the need for at least a part-time documentation specialist or coordinator.

But DP managers do not have to wait for a full-scale documentation project to begin enjoying the benefits of useful documentation if they understand that programmers, programmer/analysts, and system analysts are always creating their own unofficial, private systems and programming documentation. These notes, flow charts, and comments may be scribbled on the back of a used COBOL coding form, but they are still useful and represent many hours of thinking. They should not be wasted.

The DP manager needs to appoint one senior-level programmer or analyst as the departmental "documentation coordinator" responsible for collecting and organizing any available system documentation. This should also include memos about shop procedures and policies. The format is not important, as long as the material is organized in loose-leaf notebooks—one for each application system and one for general information. These simple notebooks are enough to start any DP shop on the road to effective and standardized documentation. People will complain that the notebooks lack organization, or are too organized, or are too detailed, or are not detailed enough, but if the information is useful, the first-level supervisors can eventually train the staff to "look in the book" first.

The notebooks should provoke enough interest in documentation coordinators to encourage them to upgrade and perhaps standardize the documentation. Standards will eventually develop, and the notebooks will be useful for both training and reference. Management need only give the professional staff a start!

MANAGING FOR PRODUCTIVITY

For middle and upper DP management, the daily routine is often made up of a series of decisions which determine both the short-term and long-term direction of the department or section. These decisions are based on such factors as cost, company priority, and available labor. However, managers should also consider the fact that their decisions can and will affect total departmental productivity.

Just as important as the daily decisions, is the total management philosophy. Whether managers or supervisors know it or not, their attitudes toward people, systems, and their own positions will help determine not only the morale of the department but the productivity as well. As mentioned before, productivity is not merely a function of the number of hours spent by staff members—it is also directly related to the management style and philosophy. There are at least six management policies that will encourage productivity.

First, a manager should always try to choose the path of least risk. In production support work, such as setting up reruns or special processing cycles, a manager or supervisor must sometimes choose between several options suggested by the technical staff. All other factors being equal, the smart manager should choose the path or option that offers the least risk. What seems like a shortcut may prove to be a costly mistake that will require additional labor or resources. The job of "fixing the fix" is far too common in data processing.

Those professionals who have a strong inner need to try their hunches and test new ideas should generally be allowed to do so, but not during critical production or development periods. Innovation is indeed a basic feature of data processing, but every supervisor, manager, or director must realize that a new technique is not justified simply by virtue of its novelty. *Conservatism* is not a dirty word in data processing, as long as it is tempered with reason and facts.

The second management technique is to define areas of responsibility carefully. Writers who describe modern organizational life usually mention that a great deal of time is wasted by both management and line staff in trying to unload distasteful responsibilities and win more interesting ones. In a large data processing organization perhaps too much time is spent trying to decide who is responsible for what! How far does the authority of the data base administrator go? Are systems and programming responsible for checking production JCL listings? Does system software have a duty to help the payroll programmers with their strange I/O problem? Can the corporate DP staff dictate to the Kansas City branch what type of minicomputer they can buy and what software to use? Is the DP manager responsible for the new word processing system that marketing just purchased without consulting him?

The list of examples could go on forever, as could the time wasted by professionals and managers while arguing, debating, plotting, and scheming to win their own positions. As a result, in addition to the productive time lost by the contestants, their employees become confused as to who is responsible for what. Senior management must take the lead and demand fast and equitable decisions when these jurisdictional disputes arise. Even though it may be very difficult, there should be no doubt about who is indeed responsible, and this attitude should extend to all areas of the organization.

A third policy to encourage productivity is to require all managers, system analysts, and senior staff members to use written communication for important matters. The old adage, "If it hasn't been put on paper, it hasn't been said" is true more often than not. Any observer of a data processing installation will notice valuable time wasted because the employees are confused by verbal instructions, the directions are incomplete, or the user simply had not thought through his or her original request. Yes, it is easy to overdo the emphasis upon written communication and consequently lower productivity by tying up personnel with paperwork, but a reasonable approach to written communication will go a long way toward providing the staff with useful and well-defined instructions. Employees who are not sure of what to do cannot be very productive, and relying primarily upon verbal communication is one frequent cause of low productivity.

A fourth management policy which pays large dividends in terms of successful projects is to emphasize that knowledge not be centralized in the management ranks. Too often—in data processing and in other professions—the managers and supervisors tend subconsciously to retain knowledge about events, people, systems, and plans, which should be communicated to the staff. Perhaps this feeds the manager's ego or sense of power, but most technical and nonsensitive business information can and should be disseminated to all qualified employees. As mentioned before, a manager who presents an image as a "superstar" is not always functioning at a true management level and may be trying to consolidate information and knowledge in his or her own position rather than develop the staff. Such managers actually spend a good part of their time acting as "errand boys" because they refuse to give the necessary authority and knowledge to others.

A final policy which matches the concept of "decentralized knowledge" is that of "egoless management," an extremely difficult and controversial management attitude which, if used properly, can dramatically boost morale, productivity, and professional performance. This attitude must be strongly held by those who are in a position to establish a management style. Managers can assume a style that builds events, procedures, and people around them personally ("ego management") or a style that allows their employees to help in the decision making, planning, and organization and lets them take the credit ("egoless management"). The manager in the latter case thus becomes more of a teacher, coach, or resource and should know when to step in with firm authority and when to step back and let the staff bask in the glory. An egoless manager is not "one of the boys"—rather, he or she manages the people and situations in such a way as to develop the professional staff, give them responsibility, and allow them to function at full productivity as "partners" rather than employees. For the "egoless manager," title and position are secondary. His or her first concern is always the total performance of the section and the job satisfaction of the staff. Managers not obsessed with their positions can give more time to managing projects, assignments, and people, rather than attempting to control the environment so as to emphasize their personal success. In terms of true productivity and positive morale, an "egoless" manager may not appear to be a "superstar" but is definitely the best one for the job. Developing "egoless" managers can often be the most positive single step toward increasing productivity in the data processing profession.

3

Personnel Management: DP Style

Data processing people *are* somewhat different, at least in terms of the technical demands made on them and the requirements for success in this complicated and sometimes frustrating field. The unique environment of a busy data processing installation requires characteristics such as tenacity, inquisitiveness, and the ability to handle both technical and business problems at the same time. Many DP managers, however, fail to realize that these technical people—who may appear to be lost in their own world of "bits, bytes, and reruns"—are still employees, and people, and have the same basic human needs of other employees.

It is just as important to correctly manage the "people" aspect of data processing as it is to manage the development of the new order entry system. People, after all, are still the means by which that new application system can be developed on time and within budget. Employees who are dissatisfied, poorly motivated, or not fully productive will have difficulty completing their assignments and will be a constant source of trouble for management. One essential way to develop satisfied and productive employees is to create a meaningful and practical "human relations" program.

Unfortunately, in the real world of data processing, DP managers cannot always look to their personnel departments for that program—it is usually up to the DP managers themselves. Corporate personnel policies must deal with a wide range of clerical, industrial, professional, and managerial employees and can rarely focus enough attention upon the unique data processing environment. Even if a personnel director had the desire to develop such a specific program, he or she might not have enough experience with data processing employees to deal with their special problems.

The only realistic solution is for the senior data processing staff to focus on personnel issues with the same attitude they might bring to a new file access method—seeing it as a challenge that can be mastered with enough thought, planning, and effort. Usually, a personnel policy developed by a data processing section can be implemented in the data processing department, if not integrated into the company's personnel plan. Even if all aspects of a good, sound DP personnel policy are not approved for the entire company, senior company management and the personnel department will be made more aware of the special needs of data processing employees and the concern of the senior DP executives over personnel issues.

JOB DESCRIPTIONS ARE IMPORTANT

The immediate response of most data processing people to the subject of job descriptions is a snicker, if not an outright laugh. "You can't describe my job" is a frequent retort because many people in this profession believe their work environment is so varied that any description is inaccurate, incomplete, or both. The obvious exceptions to this attitude are those in well-defined positions such as data entry or computer operations. Perhaps this feeling is partially valid, but it is even more true that reasonable position descriptions are the key to developing any logical personnel or human relations program. Also, managers find it difficult to manage or supervise employees if they are not sure what those staff members do with their time! Salary actions are difficult if they are not based on promotions or evaluations which are in turn based on accurate job and position descriptions.

Computer operators function at three levels of experience and technical skill. A computer operator trainee is still learning but can perform such actions as mounting tapes and disk packs, loading production jobs, and operating peripheral input and output devices. Trainees work under the direction of an experienced operator and require at least a minimum of supervision at all times. They are seldom allowed to run either production or complex test jobs themselves, unless the supervising or training operator has seen them perform the action before. Most trainees have some experience in the operations section, or perhaps in the tape library, and are at least partially familiar with the data processing environment and the organization. Data entry operators are often an excellent source of operator trainees and will in the future, become even better sources for those companies reducing data entry positions by using on-line systems with data entry in the user departments.

After several months of experience and satisfactory progress, the operator trainee should be promoted to a full computer operator. This job description should include the requirements of running production jobs and tests and handling normal operating system and hardware problems without supervision. After approximately a year, the computer operator should be promoted to one of several senior positions. Depending upon the complexity of the shop, one, two, or even three senior operator positions with slightly different job descriptions may be needed. A small single CPU environment may need only one senior-level operator, whereas a large, multi-CPU installation with complex teleprocessing networks may need up to three levels of senior operators. Job descriptions can be defined both by observation and by asking the senior operating staff for the responsibilities and typical job duties that separate them from the lower-level computer operators. Perhaps the senior operators have more contact with the programming or systems software staff or communicate and work with the vendor technicians during service calls. In many cases, their responsibilities will overlap with the operations supervisor, and they may assume supervisory responsibility in the absence of the shift supervisor.

The titles of these positions are unimportant. The major point is that each position should have its own job description, which can be studied and evaluated and compared with other levels of operators. Once the differences in day-to-day responsibilities are noted, it is a fairly easy matter to create meaningful job descriptions. Indeed, one reason that DP managers complain about the difficulty of developing meaningful job descriptions is that they seldom ask their employees to describe their daily activities!

Operations shift supervisors and managers need their own job descriptions and can usually be asked to develop their own. The emphasis should be on the managing, supervising, and planning activities. A manager or director will also have some responsibility for compiling the budget and long-range planning activities.

Although tape librarians and data entry operators have well-defined job descriptions, many installations have people in categories such as peripheral operators (running a burster or decollator), customer contact representative (answering phone calls from users and relaying messages), and operations assistants (delivering reports and picking up data entry work). These employees typically have one-line job descriptions, which are an indirect cause of low productivity. A person whose primary job duty is to deliver reports will certainly find time when there are no reports to deliver. These positions need secondary job responsibilities which can be assumed when the primary responsibility is done. A peripheral operator could be assigned to help the shift supervisor finish the daily paperwork or deliver test results. A customer services representative may help balance reports during peak production times. Complete job descriptions will often provide a department or section with additional power by encouraging management to look upon employees as resources rather than performers of restricted tasks. Formalized job descriptions are an excellent way to expand an employee's role in the organization and provide him or her with exposure to more aspects of the department.

The systems and programming area is more complex and fluid than the operations section, since there are more levels of positions and more people involved in a wider range of activities. Also, trends in the 1980s will lead to increases in the number and type of people in the systems and programming area, such as the data base administrator concept, which was virtually unknown a few years ago.

The most common type of activity in most DP shops is, of course, programming. However, this "catchall" phrase has been so overworked that each DP manager must develop his or her own set of job descriptions to fit the company and staff. The following information is a suggested procedure to classify and standardize the more typical programming and systems development professionals.

To provide an adequate career path for programmers, and to define common programming activities accurately, one must consider up to six stages of programming experience, capability, and expertise. A programmer/trainee has some educational background or experience and always works under the direction of a programmer or supervisor who is responsible for both the trainee's work and rate of learning. The trainee's duties should include coding, compiling, and developing operating system interfaces as required. The job description should always include a statement indicating that the employee is expected to learn basic programming skills as well as installation procedures through on-the-job training, formal instruction, or some combination of both. Some form of this last statement should be included in most other systems and programming positions. Each member of the professional staff should know that part of the job description is to continue learning and developing and in that way eventually to become a more valuable and productive employee.

After six months to a year of satisfactory performance, programmer trainees should be promoted to programmer positions in which they can work on more complex and sophisticated modules. Their work assignments may now include changes to systems, and they may now be expected to start learning to understand an integrated system. A programmer should be able to function with minimum supervision and without highly detailed specific instructions. Technically, the programmer should know or at least begin to understand file access procedures and basic data base manipulations, if the shop uses a data base management system.

Although some shops use the term "senior programmer" to describe the next step in a career path, few installations have a true senior programmer role which mainly involves working with the technical details of programming and operating system interfaces. A more realistic term is the programmer/analyst, a person who has mastered basic programming skills and can now deal with application system interfaces as well as individual program modules. The job description of a programmer/analyst should include a goal of learning a specific application system from both the technical and business aspects. This may include some user contact, usually under the direction of a supervisor or systems analyst. A programmer/analyst should be able to handle both maintenance and development projects.

It is interesting to note that with the programmer/analyst position, and with increasingly higher level jobs, the description of actual duties and the skill requirements tend to merge. In reality, staff members promoted to or hired as programmer/analysts will have a wide range of abilities, and the hiring manager must gauge the applicant's potential in addition to evaluating past job performance. Trying to estimate potential is one of the more difficult aspects of employee selection.

After about two years as a programmer/analyst, the professional who has shown both responsibility and technical skills should be promoted to a senior programmer/analyst position. This job description will include supervising and instructing the more junior members of the section, participating in system development and maintenance decisions, and taking responsibility for projects requiring the efforts of several individuals. Smaller DP shops may even use a senior programmer/analyst as a project leader with some management responsibilities, although more often than not the typical programmer/analyst promoted to a senior position is not trained to handle first-level management responsibility.

Medium- and large-sized installations need two additional programming titles and job descriptions for professionals who have no desire to be project leaders, who have no current opportunity to apply for such supervisory roles, or who lack the management potential to become supervisors. These additional titles will also give recognition to those individuals who are beyond the senior programmer/analyst role and who may be tempted to leave the organization for better career opportunities. Perhaps these titles and job descriptions will not completely satisfy those professionals, but they will allow the company and department to promote those people and give them adequate salary adjustments.

The two positions are "lead programmer/analyst" and "senior lead programmer/analyst." The job descriptions should include all of the tasks assigned to a senior programmer/analyst, with several additional responsibilities, such as acting as project leader in the absence of that individual, handling special projects assigned by the DP manager or programming supervisor, and acting as a technical expert for the programming staff. Another productive way to use a lead programmer/analyst is to make him or her a "floater," a highly experienced professional who can be assigned to specific project teams or groups to help solve problems, provide advice, and help meet critical deadlines.

All job descriptions for trained programming people should include some degree of coding and direct "hands on" experience, although the amount of time spent in detail-coding will be reduced as the person progresses career-wise, and develops skills such as system design and project management. In the real world of data processing, however, there are always times when the senior-level technical staff must pitch in and help meet a deadline or solve a particular problem. It becomes a touchy management situation to ask a professional to perform a task that is clearly not a part of his or her formal job description; making sure that coding is a part of the job description will help prevent that problem. Also, it helps show the junior staff that coding is not necessarily an activity that separates the junior-level people from the "privileged" senior staff.

Traditional job classifications separate the true systems analyst from the more technical programming positions. A systems analyst usually has a programming background and also a detailed knowledge of the company or business application. His or her job duties include working with users to help define problems, new applications, and procedures. He or she will usually interact with a wide variety of people in the user departments, such as managers and clerical-level personnel who may actually use the system and will work directly with DP managers, project leaders, and programmers. A systems analyst will help define requirements, design a technical system or procedure to help accomplish the business goals, and monitor the entire system development cycle. The typical product of a systems development project is a written, formal proposal, created by the systems analyst and reviewed in detail by all concerned parties. The ability to listen is essential for a successful systems analyst. Since each DP installation has slightly different duties for system analysts, the DP manager must observe and work with the current staff to develop an accurate job description that reflects the true environment of the shop. The larger installations may have several titles, such as junior systems analyst, systems analyst, and senior systems analyst.

The project leader is usually the first-level DP supervisor, although small shops need only the position of programming and systems supervisor. The first-level supervisor is responsible for programmers assigned to a specific application or technical area, and his or her duties include monitoring projects as a representative of management, supervising staff and making hiring and salary recommendations, and helping evaluate changes to the production systems.

Second- and third-level DP management varies so much between installations that it is not feasible to discuss particular positions since the job responsibilities depend primarily upon the organization of the data processing department.

As senior DP management tries to discover ways to improve the productivity and morale of the professional staff, they will use more and more paraprofessionals. These are people who usually do not have formal DP training but can successfully perform many tasks now being done by the programmers or analysts at significantly less cost.

Job descriptions are extremely important for paraprofessionals whose initial hiring justification is to perform one task, such as filing, or checking large numbers of production listings. In many cases, a paraprofessional can quickly develop enough skills to perform more tasks than originally assigned. For example, a clerk who was hired to review production listings and reports can be taught to submit the more routine production support jobs or assist programmers in making large numbers of specific, well-defined changes to program modules. Data processing as a profession has given the technical staff too many duties that can be done by the less trained—and lower paid—people. Frequent revision and expansion of job descriptions of paraprofessionals can go a long way toward rectifying that costly business mistake.

Position descriptions for all those in data processing should be examined regularly because the environment and company policy may change enough to justify new positions and responsibilities as well as to eliminate others. This review should be done with members of the staff who are in the particular job category. The interaction between employee and manager will not only help develop more accurate and consistent job descriptions, but will also help open up lines of communication that may previously have been closed.

CAREER-PATH PLANNING AND REVIEW PROCEDURES

Formalized job descriptions will provide the DP senior staff with enough information to set up adequate career development paths for the existing staff and future employees. Too often in job interviews, an applicant may ask about the career path in a company and receive an answer that is mumbled, evasive, and involves a quick look at the organizational chart. The structure of a department is not, one must emphasize, a substitute for a professional career path; most experienced DP professionals know this. Some data processing managers never learn it.

In both operations and programming, managers need to show employees a chart with job titles and a career "ladder" of options and possibilities. The chart should be prepared with the same care and consideration that would be used to make a presentation to the vice-president—it should reflect a true concern for professionals and their potential growth within the company.

Some companies require the approval of the personnel department for job titles and position descriptions, especially in the larger, multi-division and multi-location corporations which have more than one DP installation. This requirement may affect the career path plan and may force the data processing department to follow an older, formally approved set of titles which are inappropriate for the current situation. It may be possible, however, to use the new job titles in career path planning while retaining the traditional job descriptions and titles for salary review and other official purposes.

Formal salary reviews are usually performed once a year on the anniversary date of the employee, but many perceptive DP managers now believe that a once-a-year performance review in not enough. A far better plan is to have a performance review at least once between the yearly salary reviews so the professional has a well-defined opportunity to discuss his or her progress with management, and so management has an equal chance to point out problems and successes. An even better method is to hold reviews at four-month intervals.

Although the procedure, style, and format of the yearly salary review is usually fixed by company policy, a DP management team can often receive permission to develop a more appropriate review procedure for their own department, which may include a form to relate job performance with the actual day-to-day duties of the various job classifications. One reason that first-level supervisors may balk at the concept of "four-month performance reviews" is the difficulty associated with using a generalized, company-wide form to evaluate technical DP people. Developing a special DP department form will eliminate that problem. Of course, the evaluation form itself will need to be reviewed as the first- and second-line supervisors gain more experience with the form and the new procedure.

A basic performance evaluation for a programmer or programmer/ analyst should include at least three technical areas:

1 Primary and secondary languages, including proficiency in reading code, knowledge of file access methods, problem solving ability, speed of coding, and general ability of coding.
2 Operating system fundamentals, including control cards (JCL), special features, problem solving ability, and concern for efficiency.
3 Application system knowledge of production or development systems.

The final section of the form should evaluate the professional's ability to follow instructions, complete assignments on time, understand the general project or task goals, and perform successfully as a member of the data processing staff. The form should have spaces for additional comments by the reviewer, the person approving the review, and the employee himself.

The most common type of evaluation consists of a rating scale with a range from 0 to 5. It is a good idea to follow the same rating scale (either numerical or verbal) used by the official company review form.

Promotions will naturally come faster to the less-experienced professionals new to data processing, but each member of the department, with a few exceptions, should expect a valid promotion and title change at least every two years. The exceptions include relatively fixed positions, such as data entry operators and managers. Professionals in other areas, such as systems and programming, should always be considered for promotion, and such an event should be publicly recognized. Obviously, first-line management positions are limited, and the senior employees need a meaningful career path which offers growth and new challenges. A company which has no desire to create such senior positions is admitting its failure to retain the experienced staff.

Salary actions and policy are directly related to company personnel policies, and the only input a DP manager can reasonably make is to provide the personnel office with current information on the local salary structure. DP executives should regularly examine salary surveys and newspaper advertisements to keep in touch with the local and regional job market. It is not realistic to expect a personnel department to be in tune with a rapidly changing data processing salary situation, and DP managers who leave salary schedules entirely to the personnel department may find themselves no longer competitive with other local companies in the race to attract and hire good technical talent. Every good DP manager who has final hiring responsibility should send for all salary surveys advertised in the trade press.

HUMAN RELATIONS TRAINING FOR SUPERVISORS

The weakest elements of most data processing departments are the management skills of the first-line supervisors—or perhaps the lack of such skills! Project leaders are usually promoted from the staff and find themselves for the first time asked to manage other people, including their former colleagues. Many times they have no chance to work with the previous project leader in a transitional period and are simply told to "take over!" Although some larger companies provide an occasional management or supervisory training program, the typical project leader is left to fend for himself and learn supervisory skills on a trial-and-error basis.

Part of this "trial-and-error" self-teaching involves an unconscious tendency to imitate the style of one's manager and others in supervisory positions. More often than not, the imitation will result in an ineffectual project leader—the odds are great that the person chosen as the model will himself not be a trained, effective supervisor. Management has not been one of the strong points of the data processing profession! Perhaps in five or 10 years this situation will change, but smart DP executives today will understand this problem and attempt to rectify it as part of their personnel management program.

Newly appointed first-line supervisors need instruction in human relations and management skills, not necessarily in the activity known traditionally as "project management." Project management is actually learned through experience in being part of major development projects, which is still a comparatively rare experience. Of course, there are several useful books on project management techniques and some excellent (but expensive) seminars, but successful project leaders usually report that experience is still the ultimate teacher. If a company cannot provide successful on-the-job project management experience, a senior-level person who will be in charge of a major development project should be considered for an outside seminar. Even at a direct cost of several thousand dollars, the company will save the potentially higher indirect cost of mistakes and management errors in a large-scale development effort.

Management training is another matter, however, and can be learned from more formal and structured training programs. Certainly, experience is an excellent teacher, but most companies simply cannot afford to allow first-line supervisors to "experiment" through trial and error on their employees—the errors can be disastrous! Whereas the data processing organization usually hands an employee a new office key and says "Congratulations, you are now a manager!" the medical profession does not hand a hospital orderly a scalpel and say "Congratulations, you are now a brain surgeon!"

The ideal solution is to send a first-line supervisor to a seminar or in-house course taught by an experienced manager trained to teach human relations and management techniques. A less ideal procedure is to set up an internal training program which includes discussions with other supervisors (at least several to insure a wide variety of experiences), reading books on management theory and practice (preferably purchased by the company for this purpose), and self-evaluation through conferences with the supervisor's manager. The important point is to realize that management skills are not natural to most people and must be developed through training. The sooner the training starts, the better for the supervisor, his other employees, and the company.

COMMUNICATIONS

Another technique for developing a sound personnel management policy is to open the lines of communication between the employees and the management staff and to ensure that the communication works both ways. Meetings set up to improve communications too often become sessions in which the manager does all the talking, and consequently learns nothing. The employee walks away more disgruntled than before the session. *Managers need to know when to keep their mouths firmly shut and their ears firmly open.*

Two-way communication is important and can be justified not only by the benefits which accrue from allowing employees to speak their minds but also by the fact that employees are often the source of excellent suggestions. The manager or supervisor who believes that he or she always knows best is not only creating morale problems by not allowing two-way communication, but is also missing potentially sound ideas from the section staff. The group's productivity will suffer, and he or she may be unable to explain the reasons to management.

The wrong way to increase two-way communication is to hold a meeting and ask the employees to suddenly "open up." Most likely, the staff will sit quietly and not respond. Communication is stilted or even impossible when employees feel themselves part of an adversary relationship. A program to build up lines of two-way communication involves several techniques which can be implemented over a period of time, and this slow, careful process will both open the communication lines and help keep them open.

One method is to insist that the first-line supervisors hold a weekly status or progress meeting. The purpose will be to exchange information about the group activities and share problems and solutions. Although the supervisor will act as the leader and monitor the discussion, more and more of the actual reporting should be done by the team members. A supervisor who talks for 30 minutes and then closes the meeting with a quick "Are there any questions?" is not holding a meeting; rather, he is giving a lecture. If a supervisor feels that the staff is not ready to make verbal reports or discuss problems intelligently, he or she should encourage them to improve their skills in this area through individual discussions. Verbal communication, after all, is one of the most important activities in most data processing environments and needs to be continually improved. Any programmer or programmer/analyst should be able to report the status of his or her projects or tasks. Professionals and managers alike must learn when to talk and when to listen.

Another technique is to allow communication between the employee and the supervisor's manager—skipping one level in the normal chain of command. Some companies provide yearly interviews at that level, but participants usually report unsatisfactory results. In many situations the employee hardly knows the person in the next level of the organization—other than merely saying "hello"—and cannot reasonably be expected to talk frankly and honestly. Sometimes the employee will take the safe approach and tell the manager what he or she thinks the manager wants to hear! The solution is to allow informal interchange between employees and the second-level manager on a more-or-less routine basis. This can be accomplished by encouraging managers to "bypass" the chain of command to gain detailed information, and allowing employees to sit in on meetings between supervisor and managers when the subject is of joint concern. A manager does not always need to ask a supervisor to ask a programmer or operator—the manager can ask the employee himself.

Department or section meetings should be held at least once a quarter and the department manager should make a formal presentation of the department's activities and goals. This gives employees another opportunity to ask questions and inform management of their concerns. Questioning in a group situation can be encouraged by giving an employee positive feedback regardless of the merits of the employee's question. This attitude will inspire other staff members to ask questions and may provoke interesting discussions.

If the employees in a given department are having a hard time communicating with management, it may be due to a formalized atmosphere which simply does not lend itself to free two-way communication. The atmosphere in any particular unit is usually determined by the general company atmosphere as well as the personalities of the management and staff and can rarely be changed. It is possible, however, to provide more informal opportunities for discussions in a neutral area. A "brown bag" lunch once a month is one technique to help develop communications in a more friendly, neutral atmosphere. The purpose is not to make "buddies" of the managers and employees, but to give both sides a chance to talk about work-related matters (or anything else) in a situation less threatening than a formal meeting. This informal approach to communication is more difficult for a manager to handle, but any reasonably proficient manager or supervisor should be able to encourage free discussion. The results will be well worth the time.

Several companies, with varying degrees of success, have instituted a written company-wide suggestion program. One danger is the employees who have had their recommendations turned down or disregarded by their supervisors may turn to the company suggestion program as a means of bypassing the chain of command. In most situations, however, a reasonably administered written suggestion program—perhaps with a token monetary award—can be a useful tool to improve communications in the entire organization.

The final step in any plan to improve communications between employee and management is to make sure that each employee has "stand-alone" time with his or her supervisor. Section meetings and memos are no substitute for regular, direct, face-to-face private meetings between employee and supervisor. Each staff member should be able to count on a prearranged time slot, when he or she can interact with the supervisor and clear up misunderstandings, define problems and solutions, and discuss those matters that are best saved for employee-manager meetings.

DIFFICULT SITUATIONS

A busy data processing environment is particularly prone to situations in which management wants one thing and employees want another. It may be in terms of weekend or night-shift work schedules, job assignments, or even mandatory overtime to meet a deadline. A software programmer, for example, may be asked to work nights for a week to test the next system release, and a programmer/analyst may be told to help with a maintenance task when he or she would prefer to help design the new inventory control system. The problem can often arise in job assignments, since most programmers and programmer/analysts are hired as "general purpose" staff and not for any specific area or project. Those who are hired for a specific assignment will be moved to another project when the original assignment is completed. An even more frequent source of friction arises when a programmer is required to help support the production application systems at night or on weekends. This can have anywhere from a minimal to a devastating effect upon a programmer's personal life. How these situations are handled from a human relations standpoint can sometimes make the difference between a reasonably satisfied employee and one who is ready to leave the company.

There are four techniques which will help DP management handle an unpleasant work assignment or job requirement.

First, the middle-level management must discover the general attitude toward that requirement in the current staff. If most programmers in a shop react negatively toward production support, for example, other programmers will quickly pick up this feeling and look upon production support as something to avoid at all costs. Only very rare individuals will be able to resist such a general department feeling, although most professional staff will state publicly that they have an open mind and do not prejudge those matters.

If the department has strong negative feelings about certain activities, management should try to change this attitude through the efforts of the first- and second-level managers. Supervisors who have direct and frequent contact with employees must examine their personal attitudes. Do they occasionally make disparaging remarks about the task, or do they treat the assignment as punishment, or a matter of bad luck? Do they approach the subject as if it were unpleasant? If the answer is yes, the supervisor or manager must try to look at the assignment in a new and more positive light. Unpleasant situations are often made worse if managers add their own negative feelings— even unconsciously—to an already negative departmental attitude.

The second step is to make sure that all employees and the supervisory staff realize the importance of the assignment to the department and the company. Making changes in a tricky accounts payable program may not be exciting and may even be frustrating, but it will have a direct impact upon the accounts payable section and perhaps help the operation or the company. The staff involved should know the reasons and benefits to be derived from the task and should not just be told "This is your job!" The few minutes spent telling employees the positive consequences of their actions for the company will be repaid by having more motivated employees.

A programmer on the production support team must be told the effects of not having warehouse invoices done by 6:00 A.M.—for example, 75 warehouse employees may not be able to start working or, if overnight batch production is not done by 10:00 A.M., a bank might not be able to start its on-line day teller processing. Even the most frustrating and unpleasant job in data processing has its good points and significance, and the employee should understand the good along with the bad. This information is best passed along to the entire group, even those who are not yet involved in that unpleasant assignment.

The third technique is to hold a private, individual session with the employee and review all aspects of the job or task. Sometimes merely giving the staff member a chance to express doubts or feelings in a secure atmosphere will do much to alleviate those negative feelings. At the same time, the supervisor should not minimize the problems and disadvantages of the assignment—they will be evident soon enough and a lie will only make the situation worse.

The last technique is to always be aware of the staff member who is not entirely satisfied and be alert to slight behavioral or attitudinal changes which may indicate a serious morale and motivational problem. It is then time for another individual meeting. Employees should realize that their managers do care about their job-related emotions and feelings. This "caring" attitude will form the foundation of a solid human relations program.

Difficult situations can also arise when personal or family problems interfere with an employee's job performance. A personality clash between a staff member and supervisor can also contribute to a poor attitude and equally poor job performance. Data processing people should be handled as any other employees, with the manager or supervisor attempting to rectify the situation if it is in his or her power. If the problem concerns the employee's personal life, there is nothing the manager can do except lend a sympathetic ear.

Unsatisfactory performance on the job is another difficult area that must be approached with both tact and firmness. Obviously, the staff member must be told specifically what the deficiencies are and how he or she can correct them. The second-level manager must verify that all supervisors can provide a poorly motivated employee with suggestions for improvement and can approach a bad review situation with a helpful attitude. At the same time, however, the DP staff member in question must realize the situation, understand the particular problems with his or her actions, and know the consequences if he or she does not improve. Any supervisor who must give such a bad review should discuss the procedure with a more experienced manager who can give some advice on what to expect.

A human relations program should also give the employee a chance to answer criticisms and poor reviews, both during the review process and whenever the manager finds a reason to downgrade the employee's performance. After all, experienced DP managers have for years reported instances in which supervisors either misread an employee's job performance, did not understand his or her work environment, or indirectly caused poor job performance by their own mismanagement of that individual. In the real world, not much can be done to rectify such situations without entirely destroying the credibility of the supervisor. One excellent management practice is for the second- and third-level managers to question in detail all unsatisfactory reviews and demand concrete examples of poor job performance. A complete discussion between the supervisor and his or her manager should be required before any poor review is approved by management. All supervisors or first-level managers who seldom give good reviews should be carefully reviewed themselves.

REVIEWING DATA PROCESSING EMPLOYEES

Although managers usually have definite criteria with which to evaluate staff members with well-defined jobs such as data entry and computer operators, they may throw up their hands in despair at the complex and seemingly intuitive job of evaluating programmers and systems analysts. After all, programmers cannot be rated by the number of lines of code produced, and systems analysts cannot be measured by the number of flow charts they create! Some executives state that the only type of employee that is more difficult to evaluate properly than a programmer is another manager.

The reviewing process need not involve that much intuition and outright "guessing" if the supervisory staff is willing to follow a detailed and logical methodology. The result of this process may not be quite what is required by the official company review form, but it can be easily adapted to match almost any evaluation form or company requirement. Considerations other than those mentioned in this methodology should be used at the discretion of the reviewer. One important but usually unspoken consideration is the estimated value of the employee to the department, both now and in the future; that is, certain employees may be rated higher than their actual performance if they are judged to be future key members of a specific section or team and would react very negatively if given only an "average" review. This method should be reserved for special situations which justify an adjustment in the normal reviewing process.

This general methodology involves six steps.

First, employees should be given copies of the blank review form several weeks in advance of the review date so they can rate themselves. This technique will uncover situations in which employees and supervisors have serious disagreements and will give staff members a chance to undertake the very valuable practice of self-evaluation. The supervisor should not see the employee's self-rating until after his or her own official review has been approved by management. There is too much chance that a careless or lax supervisor will use the employee's self-rating as the basis for his or her own evaluation.

Second, the supervisor should list all the accomplishments of the individual, with the major accomplishments described in detail and the minor or short-range tasks summarized by type and degree of difficulty. This data should be evident from the weekly or monthly management reports. If the supervisor cannot create the list from available written information, the second-level manager needs to examine the department or section management reporting system because the supervisor apparently does not know what his or her employees have been doing!

Third, along with the list of accomplishments, the supervisor should consider the problems faced by the employee in the past reviewing period. Perhaps he or she was continually interrupted by other staff members asking questions or requesting assistance or had great difficulty getting adequate test time. Was the inventory control system six months late because the new merchandise manager kept changing the requirements? Was the new accounts payable system the first true production system ever designed by this new systems analyst?

It is impossible to fairly evaluate any staff member without considering in detail all of the problems—both major and minor—the employee had to surmount in order to accomplish his or her goals.

Fourth, the supervisor will need to consider the more favorable aspects of the employee's performance in the general areas of attitude, stability, initiative, professionalism, and competence. A programmer or analyst who has shown extreme initiative, for example, should be praised for that quality. In any particular work environment and job position, of course, the personal characteristics of an employee will have different values. A high-pressure maintenance shop, for example, may place a premium on stability, whereas a development project team may emphasize initiative.

A good reviewer will always note at least one positive aspect of a person's behavior, even if the staff member is rated very poorly. This small, positive note may be enough in some cases to turn a potentially disastrous situation into one which can give the employee encouragement to improve job performance.

Fifth, the supervisor should follow his praise of the employee's accomplishments with the negative or less satisfactory aspects of his work. Any negative comments must be supported by specific examples which clearly illustrate the behavior in question. Experienced managers like to have more than one example to present to an employee, even though the official review form may have room for only one example, if any. Employees may become defensive and deny the behavior or action until they realize the supervisor has enough concrete examples to overcome any objections. These additional examples should be used only when absolutely necessary, or when it is clear that the employee does not understand the situation.

At this point, the reviewer will want to carefully consider the employee's "image," as perceived by the supervisor or manager. Some technical people are handicapped by being unable to present a professional image, even though their actual job performance may be excellent. Others in a data processing organization may not inform their supervisors of the true range of their skills and accomplishments.

In the real world of data processing, other types of personalities do exist, such as those who constantly try to impress others with their knowledge and success, even to the point of taking credit for work done by others. Some managers call these employees "political programmers" and find that they are useful in situations which involve a degree of salesmanship. Unfortunately, few data processing managers have learned to recognize this type of individual and, consequently, promote them to supervisory positions—bypassing those with less polished images who actually get the job done. The "image" of a programmer or DP professional should not affect his or her evaluation unless that image is so negative it affects daily activities. Conversely, it is the job of a good manager to separate the real achievers from those who claim they are achievers—anyone who cannot make this judgment is not suited for a managerial position.

Finally, the reviewer should compare the staff member with colleagues of similar salary grade and job classification. Despite the traditional advice from some personnel management experts that reviews should be based solely on performance, experienced first- and second-level managers have found it virtually impossible to ignore the temptation to compare employees for review purposes. Indeed, an objective comparison between staff members is necessary because company personnel policies usually require allocations of salary increases to be based partially on comparisons. That is, an employee who has a higher review rating should get a higher salary increase than an employee with a lower rating, although many factors obviously will enter into the allocation process. There is nothing wrong with a supervisor making objective comparisons of employees as long as he or she understands the role of comparisons and their limitations. Most intelligent employees realize that comparisons are inevitable, yet may insist that part of their review be based on their own accomplishments.

Establishing a logical and progressive evaluation format will tend to make personnel reviews more accurate and consistent across supervisors. Consistency is vital when the professional staff is transferred between project leaders and are reviewed by different individuals every year. Also, following a detailed methodology tends to force supervisors to justify their ratings and evaluations.

PERSONNEL MANAGEMENT SHOULD NEVER STOP

Creating an effective human relations and personnel program in data processing is not a one-time project, but rather, should be a continuing objective of any progressive DP department. The results of such a program will eventually lead to a lower turnover rate and more satisfied, productive employees.

4

Training in the 1980s

Training is definitely an important part of any DP management plan
for the 1980s, although most data processing managers still approach
training as they would a case of poison ivy. The skin has to be
scratched to relieve the itch, and the people who lack skills must be
somehow "trained." It turns out, however, that almost everyone in
the department can benefit from training and education. Since the
need for training is relatively new to a production DP environment,
managers, executives, and senior personnel are often confused by the
maze of possible training procedures. They are frustrated by the
problem and will literally jump at the first reasonable method. After
all, it is more exciting to monitor the progress of the new on-line
general ledger system than to spend time planning the training program for five rookie programmers. From a larger management perspective, of course, those five new programmers who still have trouble
signing onto the TSO terminal may represent the future of the DP

section, as well as the key to completing the new inventory-control system or budget-planning systems now in the planning stages.

One reason for the confusion surrounding training is a lack of understanding of its true purpose. Training and education should not be "fringe" benefits designed to keep people happy (although a few organizations follow that philosophy); rather, they are important techniques to increase the productivity of programmers, programmer/ analysts, system analysts, paraprofessionals, and operations personnel. In the 1980s, the costs will be too high to allow employees to stumble around in the traditional DP manner, trying to complete their assignments through on-the-job training. Instead of assuming that it takes a year for a professional to become fully productive, successful DP managers will question this long-accepted wisdom. Can the training period be shortened to nine months? How about six months? Why do professionals with computer science degrees or previous experience require so much time to learn how to do their jobs?

Obviously, the answer is that with proper training most DP staff members who have some data processing background can become fully productive in far less time. This training will not happen magically any more than a new on-line general ledger system will miraculously appear on the CRTs, courtesy of the on-line general ledger fairy. Good training requires careful planning, forceful implementation, and strong management commitment. It may not be "fun," but it is the answer to a host of problems which will erupt in the 1980s.

IS TRAINING NECESSARY?

In a small but significant number of DP installations, managers do not need to develop a training and education program, and it would actually be a waste of time to do so. They may be blessed with a fully-trained staff, or they may have an environment which minimizes the need for technical and system knowledge. Such installations can occur by accident or design, and managers who are considering starting new DP sections or revamping their current ones should carefully consider hardware and software options that reduce the importance of technical or business expertise. For example, a minicomputer with software packages for handling application systems can do a surprising amount of work and should need little technical support after installation. The organization must consider whether it can accept the limitations of the particular software application.

The technical environment will in part determine the level of training needed. A shop which uses low-level CICS macro-programming, should plan on paying extremely high salaries to attract qualified CICS programmers or should consider a detailed training program to bring non-CICS programmers up to speed in a relatively short time. A different shop, which is moving toward an easy-to-use DBMS and report-writer system, can expect reduced technical requirements for at least some of its staff. Indeed, the training and education requirements must be an important consideration when evaluating any hardware, software, or system change. Managers can no longer assume they will find technical expertise through advertisements in the Sunday newspaper.

When considering a new application system, for example, DP management must estimate both the direct and indirect costs of any necessary training. Although data processing typically buries the cost of informal training in the classic "design" or "programming" phases of a project, it is more realistic, and honest, to create a separate budget for any training effort that will take more than one-half of a work day. Simply recognizing the large amounts of training or familiarization time required for any new project will open eyes from the senior staff to the director of MIS. Most data processing organizations will be surprised to learn how much resource time and effort can be charged to training, and they will be more motivated to manage the formal training function instead of allowing the informal training effort to manage them.

For example, when planning a new feature for the order-entry system, the systems analyst or manager must consider the training and educational needs of the staff assigned to the project. Training itself can consist of browsing through a few programs, spending a week at an off-site technical seminar, or anything in between. This informal education is usually termed "familiarization" and as an indirect budget item should be given its own time estimates and placed on the project Pert chart (or whatever control method the organization uses). The formal training involves both a direct cost (seminar plus expenses) and an indirect cost (the time lost from the job). Experi-

enced managers always estimate an extra day of lost time to allow
for the day the person comes back and tells everyone up and down
the halls how much fun he had in Chicago or New York or Los
Angeles.

Of course, it is difficult if not impossible to accurately predict
time estimates and budget costs without knowing which staff members will be on the project. Traditionally, the technique has been to
either pick the "average" experienced programmer/analyst and use
him or her as the model, or select a senior staff member and use him
or her as the basis for all time and labor estimates. In the decade of
the 1980s, neither of these techniques will work. Senior analysts now
spend most of their time helping junior staff members, and the
mythical "average" person no longer exists. With the growing trend
toward paraprofessionals and the increasing number of trainees, the
"average" is becoming even more mythical. Without selecting individuals as likely candidates for the assignment and factoring in a
training cost for them, it is virtually impossible to make valid project
plans. Training and education are a basic fact of life in the 1980s and
must be recognized in all planning activities.

Make no mistake about the need for training. The companies who
deny the need for training are often the ones which need training and
education the most. The old-fashioned answer that "We can't spare
the time" is invalid from a purely economic viewpoint. Without adequate training, education, and instruction, most highly paid professionals in data processing simply cannot do their job properly. They
may get it done, but it will not be efficient or of high quality. The
key to increasing productivity and maximizing available resources is
to plan and implement a sound, businesslike, training program.

WHERE DO TRAINING PLANS COME FROM?

However tempting it is to hire an outside organization to tackle the
complex job of developing a training program, the best, most useful,
and most successful programs originate from the internal senior staff.
These veterans have learned the hardware, software, and application
systems and are the recognized experts in terms of knowledge and
experience. They know what it takes to be successful, or at least to

get the job done in a reasonable manner. They know where to find the programs, fix the logic, and how to get around the strange CICS abend that pops up only when the chairperson of the board decides to look in on the claims department. The current employees—who probably learned only through on-the-job training—may not be interested in helping develop a training plan, but they are the most qualified resources available.

The first step in developing a sound training program is to define the goals of the entire training effort, but the main objective should be to develop people who can independently handle a specific responsibility. The measure of success of a training program is not the number of hours spent in the sessions, or the professionalism of the slide presentations, or even the effort put forth by the instructor. Rather, a graduate of the in-house DP training program should be expected to become productive in one-tenth the time it would take that person to become productive through on-the-job training.

Since the ultimate goal is to become productive in a particular job category, management must define the skills necessary to be productive. The job description will help, but there is no substitute for examining the present staff. Programmer/analysts, for example, often do an amazing number of tasks that have nothing to do with either programming or classical systems analysis. They may be expected to analyze a job flow for JCL efficiencies one day and asked to explain the fields of the Gross Margin Exception Report the next day. All activities performed by people in a specific job category need to be listed and defined, even if they are not a part of their official job description.

Employees who are considered successful are the best ones to observe when trying to analyze the skills needed in a job category. They will have individual weaknesses which must be considered, but in general, they can be studied easily and will serve as useful models. Managers should always ask such people to define the skills and knowledge they feel are important.

Once the specific requirements have been defined, the manager or management team can use those objectives as criteria for developing the ingredients of a valid training program. At this point, the manager needs to centralize training responsibility in one person. Larger shops can have one or more full-time professionals in the training role, but even small installations should appoint one senior-level staff member as the training coordinator on a part-time basis. Unless the training responsibility is formally assigned to a manager or a specific staff member, it will never get done. The training and education function is not as critical as rerunning the accounts payable system to correct the duplicate invoice problem, not as satisfying as explaining to the new vice-president the importance of the data base dictionary, not as visible as helping install the badly needed on-line credit verification system, and not as much fun as working with the new accounting supervisor who just happens to be a former model. As most managers have learned the hard way, the only way to get something done that is not critical, satisfying, visible, or fun, is to assign it to a specific individual. Training may not be fun, but it must be done.

THE MACRO TO MICRO APPROACH

Managers dream of a training program that shows a new programmer the way to the restroom in the morning, and the intricacies of the sales reporting system in the afternoon—in the mistaken belief that the new employee can immediately jump into the backlog of projects waiting to be completed. The vast majority of professionals are simply not ready to comprehend the complexities of a new data processing installation. They need to understand the company or organization, the role of data processing and an overview of the application systems, especially when the interfaces between systems are complicated or undocumented. Only at that point are they ready to learn the procedures for survival in the data processing section. Only then are they ready to understand the sales reporting system and begin to make those badly needed changes. This general-to-specific method will not excite a manager who thinks hiring a new programmer is like hiring one more stock person. While the stocking and ordering processes are usually well defined and standard throughout the business world, the art and science of programming and systems design is definitely not.

The first session for any new employee should cover personnel policies relating to benefits, salary reviews, and specific company requirements. The next several sessions should cover the history and purpose of the corporation or division; organizational structure of the entire company; names, titles, and responsibilities of the senior executives; and the role of data processing in the company. Briefings could be held in a group setting with new employees from other departments if the organization is large enough to have orientation sessions on a weekly basis, or by individual arrangement with a member of the DP staff. The instructor does not have to be the employee's manager or supervisor but can be any senior-level employee who has been around long enough to know the organization, the people involved, and something about how the puzzle fits together.

Macro training recognizes that human beings are indeed social animals and require a feeling of belonging in order to develop a commitment to the company and the particular data processing position. It is always possible to skip the introduction and general company information and go straight to the technical details, but the employee is then likely to suffer serious motivational problems later on. Even if such a professional appears to be motivated and ready to jump into battle, he or she will be more of a long-term asset if the proper attitude is developed from the beginning. The time to worry about keeping employees is when they are first hired, not when they suddenly show up in three-piece suits and ask to take two-hour lunch breaks.

During the orientation sessions, the instructor can distribute any written information about the corporation, such as annual reports, sales brochures, and company-wide memos. Written material will help the employee relate to the company if it is explained, rather than handed to the new person in a package with the casual comment, "These will tell you something about the company."

A final part of the macro training plan should be to introduce the professional to outside managers who have significant contact with the data processing section. The programmer who will be assigned to the inventory control section should formally meet the merchandise control manager and some of the key staff, since he or she will be involved either directly or indirectly with the people responsible for the inventory control function. The new computer operator should meet several of the people who will use the results of his or her production runs. Formal introductions are important and should be performed gradually over several weeks so the new employee is not overwhelmed with names and faces the first week. If data processing is a service function in the business and scientific world, then employees should at least know who they are serving.

PROCEDURAL TRAINING

The common programming languages, such as COBOL and PL/I are known as procedural languages, in that the programmer uses a well-defined language to develop a procedure to accomplish a specific purpose. Whether it is updating an on-line sales file, or transmitting an accounting report to a specific terminal, the process still depends upon a procedure. Interestingly enough, most of the daily activities of professional and nonprofessional data processing personnel consist of following repetitive procedures to accomplish their goals. And even more interesting is the fact that many DP managers never realize that procedures and techniques are often unique to an installation or application system and new staff members spend an unbelievable amount of time stumbling around trying to discover them. On-the-job training and observation of other staff members will eventually teach most of those procedures to a new employee, but in a very inefficient and haphazard manner. The decade of the 1980s will be no place for the inefficient or haphazard.

Some specific examples of techniques and procedures that vary from organization to organization are:

1   Updating source and object modules.
2   Authorizing source library changes.
3   Installing production changes.
4   Documenting problems and questions.
5   Suggesting system changes and improvements.
6   Communicating with users and the operations section.
7   Following installation standards.
8   Performing standard production support tasks.
9   Filling out time accounting project reports and status reports.
10 Making friends with the right people in order to get something done.

These procedures and techniques must be taught to new employees and should also be carefully documented for future reference. One responsibility of the training coordinators should be to develop a comprehensive list of procedures for each job category. The training sessions can be scheduled individually with either the training coordinator, the employee's supervisor, or a staff member who has successfully used some of those techniques. An on-the-job training situation, in which an employee may be under pressure to accomplish a goal, does not provide the proper milieu for developing the most efficient and businesslike methods to get the job done.

If data processing itself can be described as people following procedures, it follows that one of the most useful training aids is a procedure manual. Activities can range from correctly filling out the time reporting form to updating source modules to knowing how a programmer can report a problem to management. The format of the procedures manual to be used in training (which will be equally valuable for reference) is unimportant; indeed, there is no single "correct" style or format, and the professional staff could waste valuable weeks trying to discover this mythical "correct" format. It is more businesslike for the training coordinator to select a format, obtain the approval of management, and immediately start to document the procedures, techniques, and tricks of getting work accomplished in the particular data processing section. The only alternative to a procedures manual is for a trainee to simply ask someone for the information he or she needs. Such a policy is inefficient—it slows down the trainee and triggers unplanned interruptions of the other professionals in the group. It should not be tolerated by a management staff concerned with productivity and efficiency.

IN-HOUSE RESOURCES: MORE THAN YOU THINK

The professional education companies which produce multimedia courses on technical and data processing subjects are the most obvious resources for a training program. Their salespeople can bombard a management team with reasons for utilizing their training program. A more realistic approach is to first examine the in-house resources which are immediately available. Some large organizations rush into the training battle by contracting outside educational companies which have beautifully elaborate, well-prepared, and inspiring productions that are slick enough to warm the insides of both a Hollywood producer and a stockholder of the education company. Such video tape, audio tape, and video disk courses do have a place in a well-designed training program if the departmental budget can stand the strain and if the management team is not taking the easy way out of a confusing and frustrating situation. A better answer is to analyze the available resources and only then to consider professional education companies for specific skill needs, such as language or operating system training.

The first in-house resource is user documentation. Almost all application systems have some form of specifications, documentation, or work station packages essential to understanding the application systems from a user viewpoint. In many cases, however, the management or senior staff have never even seen the user documentation and have never considered how useful they might be in a training program. Any training plan that concentrates upon specific application systems, such as general ledger or inventory control, should present and explain the user documentation. Likewise, every data processing installation should have a library with copies of the current system user documentation.

A second resource is the internal documentation available in most data processing shops to varying degrees, usually ranging in quality from poor to totally ridiculous. Even DP organizations which loudly complain that they have no internal documentation should look around carefully for operational run sheets, job listings, balance control forms, program summaries, library listings, special processing instructions, and the ever-popular napkin from the company cafeteria with the system flow of the accounts receivable system. Except in very rare situations, some documentation will exist. It may be inadequate, outdated, incomplete, disorganized, and barely legible, but it is better than nothing and can usually be upgraded with some cooperation between a programmer and a secretary.

Using internal documentation, even if it is a visual disgrace, will help start new staff members along the road to true productivity by showing them that documentation will be an important solution to some of the productivity problems of the 1980s. Company manage-

ment can no longer afford to pay scarce professional talent to discover facts that were discovered last year or the year before—time is
money, and training with documentation is one way to minimize the
costs and maximize the accomplishments.

A third resource is the people in the data processing section itself.
Productive employees can be distinguished from unproductive ones,
partially by the extent of their knowledge and experience in the particular installation, and it is a legitimate management policy to require the experienced staff to share their experience and knowledge
with the newer people.

Too often a new programmer is told that "Jim will be glad to help
you out anytime," and Jim is casually told, "Give Fred a hand if he
has any questions." In the real world of data processing, such a well-
meaning procedure is usually a waste of time. Jim will obviously have
dozens of questions on procedures, policies, systems, and programs,
but he still has no formal, official contact. Fred knows that he had
better complete those new CRT screens for the credit verification
system by next Wednesday, and when those are tested, he should
prepare the test plan for the data base recovery project. If he has any
time left over, he will be glad to help Jim—unless, of course, he has
a dental appointment that afternoon. Fred knows what is important
in his established priorities, and Jim's education and training are simply not part of them.

Every new employee should be assigned one person of a similar
level to whom he or she can address general questions about the department and specific questions about responsibilities. While the new
employee will usually turn to an immediate supervisor for some of
those problems, the staff member still needs someone else to turn to
for advice and assistance. The questions may be technical, procedural,
or even social. To a new programmer on his or her first day, it is
important to know what time the section usually takes its mid-morn-
ing coffee break. That new programmer, after all, is a social creature
with human needs who wants to learn the social behavior of the new
organization.

Appointing one senior staff member to be a formal contact will
invariably require time from the professional's other assigned duties,
but it is time well invested. From a true management perspective, it
is justified to postpone the new credit verification CRT screens two

weeks to insure that the new analyst gets started in a reasonable amount of time. Specific deadlines are important, but so is the total departmental productivity over a one-year period, and successful managers in the 1980s must be able to balance those two needs.

The experienced staff can also teach formalized training sessions on a specific system, language, or procedure. The person selected to teach does not have to be an expert in that application or even have any teaching experience. As long as he or she has useful knowledge which can and should be passed along to the other staff members and is willing to speak informally in a group setting, that person can create a successful teaching situation. The staff being trained should not expect the world's greatest authority on inventory control to present a dazzling multimedia presentation complete with magic tricks for entertainment. The teacher should not expect to transfer knowledge the same way data is transferred from one CPU to the next; people can learn, however, by exposure to material without being asked to recall detailed facts. Useful learning will seldom, if ever, happen instantly, but in a DP department, where training sessions happen on a regular basis, learning will take place gradually and eventually justify its time and expense.

Another advantage of using in-house staff to teach the formal training sessions is that it will encourage the entire department to develop the "egoless management" idea that knowledge should be shared and not centralized. Data processing organizations throughout the world are often guilty of accidentally concentrating knowledge in a few key people, but this "key person" concept is as obsolete in the 1980s as the vacuum tube computer. Management in the 1980s—if it follows the "egoless management philosophy"—must insist that all staff members are given the opportunity to learn from the most knowledgeable people in the shop. Any data processing installation that relies upon a few select individuals to hold everything together is a ticking time bomb. The "key person" concept is convenient and does indeed feed the egos of some people, but it is a dangerous management practice in a decade of high turnover and rapidly changing technology.

The fourth resource in the company is the non-data processing departments. User sections such as accounting, finance, manufacturing, quality control, planning, marketing, sales, and payroll usually have managers or senior staff who have worked with data processing and can interact with technical people in a reasonably proficient manner. If approached in a positive way, most users will feel honored to speak to a group of DP personnel about the application systems from a user standpoint. Such talks could be general and could become part of the "macro" training sessions; or they could be specific to one system or even to a portion of one application system. Users often have detailed business expertise, which can help the technical staff better understand the system and the data flow, and which in turn should help them perform their jobs more efficiently.

MEASURING THE EFFECTS OF TRAINING

Any manager who institutes a formalized training program must measure both the cost and benefits of this expensive educational project. Most organizations require significant projects to be justified by either direct measurements or logical examination. Since data processing activities are not like an assembly line on which the number of widgets can be counted as a measure of productivity, data processing management must find indirect methods to demonstrate the true value of a training effort.

The cost of a training program is relatively easy to calculate if the organization uses a time accounting system and encourages employees to be honest in recording their time. Both the trainees and instructors should charge their time to education, with "teaching and preparation" time charged to a separate account. Once the senior staff members have gained experience in developing and preparing training materials, the time they require to organize and present a formalized training session should be significantly reduced. One note of caution should be mentioned. Senior management may be surprised and upset by the true cost, in terms of labor hours, of a good training program, unless they are properly prepared. The best way to justify such a costly project is to emphasize its value as a long-term investment which will pay dividends in terms of total departmental productivity.

The results of a good training program may be positive, but they are difficult to measure unless management uses the total performance of the data processing section as the criteria for its success. The only possible justification for spending company funds on an intangible project such as "training" is that it will help meet more of the company needs, as defined by observable, measurable criteria.

If data processing successfully trains its staff, the results should show up in these four areas:

1   Personnel turnover should be reduced.

One cause for high turnover in the data processing profession is that programmers and analysts occasionally tend to feel unproductive or even overwhelmed by their jobs. They fail more often than they succeed, and part of this failure can be blamed not only on a lack of technical knowledge, but also on a lack of knowledge regarding the application system and the project requirements. Morale drops quickly among staff who feel they must scratch and claw for every necessary fact. Professionals usually want to do a quality job the first time around. A good training program should help reduce turnover by giving the staff more opportunities for success.

2   Mistakes in both programming and systems design should be reduced.

Data processing can be described as a profession in a glass house—with a glass roof, glass floor, and large magnifying lenses in the windows. Every mistake, error, and incorrect decision made by a DP staff member is usually announced to the entire corporate world within minutes, in part because errors in computerized application systems tend to be serious and in part because people like to throw rocks at glass houses.

3   System design tasks should be more complete.

As system analysts and programmer/analysts better understand the application systems and the design process in general, their proposals and plans should become more accurate. One of the most frustrating tasks in data processing is for an analyst to try to develop a design change when he or she is unsure about the application or the user needs.

4   More projects should be done on time, and the time estimates presented to management should be more accurate.

Trained people will be better able to develop realistic project estimates, and control the project development cycle, than staff members who are unsure about their systems and requirements.

TRAINING AS A BUSINESS INVESTMENT

Training and education programs are expensive, but the only alternative to training is to let new staff members utilize the outmoded data processing practice of on-the-job training. Although many of today's managers and executives learned through on-the-job training and may feel that it has not hurt them, the best management people will recognize that the conditions of the late 1960s and early 1970s were vastly different from the rapidly changing world of the 1980s. In those early days, the computer and the data processing profession were exciting experiments in the attempt to improve business and scientific processing with electronics. In the 1980s, however, the computer has become an integral but expensive part of the total organization, and forward-looking data processing executives will learn to look on their own staff as a major company investment.

5

Recruiting in the 1980s:
The Competition Is On!

In the old days, recruiting meant putting an ad in the Sunday paper and screening resumes. The employer usually had a choice of several candidates, and the recruiting procedure—or even the lack of a procedure—didn't really matter.

The DP talent shortage of the 1980s has completely changed this picture. Even major corporations are having trouble finding qualified DP technicians and professionals, and the competition among companies is becoming fierce in the larger metropolitan areas. Some estimates predict that the programmer shortage will continue for at least five more years, but the advent of the explosion in the mini- and microcomputers industry may extend the personnel shortage well into the next decade. Even if the new "system development packages" produce a major increase in productivity during the next few years, data processing installations will still need technical people to analyze user needs and implement solutions.

Companies that fail to recognize the importance of recruiting may lose candidates to the organizations with active recruiting plans. Since many experienced DP programmers and analysts now have their choice of positions, some of these choices may be highly influenced by the effectiveness of a company's recruiting effort. Obviously, salary, position, and working conditions play a major part in a professional's choice of jobs, but his or her perception of the "professionalism" of the company—as determined by the recruiting effort—may be the deciding factor. The managers who can offer the highest salary may not be the ones who can hire the best people!

Successful recruitment of technical people is partially a job of "salesmanship," and the first step in selling anything is to define the merits of your product. The merits and benefits of a DP position—and how they are presented—may be intangible and subjective, but they still are the features that can make or break the recruiting effort.

Every DP job has its benefits, and it is up to management to emphasize those good points in newspaper ads, interviews, and discussions with potential candidates. For example, a shop that allows programmers to work on several types of application systems rather than one can stress the variety of work available. A job that involves maintenance as well as development can honestly be described as offering more variety than a position with only one type of assignment.

At the same time, it is necessary to list as honestly and accurately as possible the drawbacks and specific problems of the job. The potential employee may be a sophisticated job hunter and may very well ask direct questions about potential problems; the interviewer should be prepared to answer these questions. The answers should include a fair and accurate reply to the question as well as a restatement of the positive benefits of the job.

SHOULD YOU USE AN AGENCY?

Employment agencies are useful when there is a shortage of skilled DP professionals. Many technical people dislike the hassle and effort involved in changing jobs and prefer to let an agency do their looking and negotiating. Companies like agencies because they can search out talent that is not immediately available or is outside of the local job market.

But using an agency is not always practical. The most obvious drawback is the large fee that is usually due 30 to 90 days after hiring. A company in a tight financial bind may not allow such large expenditures and may instead require their own personnel staff to handle the recruiting. Many companies successfully use both approaches. They may list jobs through agencies but will still conduct their own recruiting effort.

The decision to use an agency should be based on the company or department budget (can it stand an agency fee this year?), the resources available in personnel (does the personnel department have the training and resources to do a thorough job?), and the shortage or surplus of experienced DP professionals in the area. Programmers and analysts usually register with an agency if they know the job market is excellent, and companies must compete to hire experienced personnel.

Any company deciding to use an agency should insist that the agency personnel screen all applicants and match them with the basic job requirements. An agency that routinely sends unscreened applicants is worthless and should be dropped. The hiring manager and personnel department must clearly state in writing the minimum requirements for the job and should only rarely allow the agency recruiters to use their own judgment. Unless the manager is confident that the agency understands both the job market and the open position, it is better to give the agency strict guidelines.

DO IT YOURSELF

Most companies can successfully recruit a technical staff if they commit at least one full- or part-time employee from the personnel department and if they prepare a detailed, positive recruiting procedure.

Before developing such a plan, it is wise to examine newspaper advertisements for the features promoted by competing companies. Successful ads usually point out the best aspects of a company or division. In some cases, the adage that "bigger is better" is indeed true and the larger, more interesting ads get the best response. It may be easier to use a "standard" newspaper ad, but the response will be better if personnel and data processing together develop an interesting, hard-hitting, and positive newspaper advertisement. The name of the game in recruiting is salesmanship, and this principle applies to selling data processing positions as well as buckets of fried chicken.

INTERVIEWERS NEED TRAINING

Most companies allow employees with little experience in hiring practices to interview and select applicants. This is just as illogical as promoting people to management slots without teaching them how to be managers.

An untrained interviewer runs the risk of missing essential information, misinterpreting statements by the applicant, and failing to give the applicant a fair picture of the position. Experienced professionals usually judge a company by their interviewers. If the interviewer himself fails to make a good impression, the applicant may decide to go elsewhere.

Unless the manager or interviewer has significant interview experience, he or she needs formal training through books or at least consultation with an experienced professional who has interviewed before. It is true, as many experienced interviewers point out, that each situation is somewhat unique, but the basic procedures of establishing positive rapport and exchanging information remain the same. The managers and supervisors who do interview for a company should meet once every few months to discuss interviewing techniques and to share suggestions.

Besides some formalized training, well-prepared interviewers should be equipped with a list of the topics to be covered. They should also prepare a secondary list of detailed questions which can be scanned quickly at the end of the interview to check that no important topics have been missed. Both the topic list and the detailed question list should be appropriate for the available position, as well as the orientation and experience of the interviewer. Under no circumstances should the interviewer be allowed to conduct an interview session extemporaneously.

If more than one person is to interview an applicant, the two interviewers should compare their topic lists and make sure there is no unplanned duplication. Data processing cannot just assume that personnel will stick to personnel issues, and personnel cannot assume that data processing will only discuss the technical side of the job. Also, comparing topic lists gives the two interviewers a chance to agree on how to handle the delicate questions of salary and the next point of contact. It is amazing how many times DP applicants report confusion between interviewers as to who said what and what they meant.

PREPARATION COUNTS!

Before the applicant arrives, personnel or data processing should prepare a folder with all available sales, marketing, and personnel information. Manufacturing companies, for example, usually have excellent brochures on their products, and most large, publicly held companies have professionally prepared yearly reports. The more information the applicant has, the more he or she will be able to relate to the company as a potential employee, or "member of the family." For example, a professional may feel lukewarm about working for the ABC Corporation, which does something or other in the retail industry, but he or she may feel more positive about working for the DEF Corporation which makes diesel generators, employs 750 people, is active in the Red Cross blood program, and has a yearly picnic at the amusement park.

It is especially important to give the applicant written information on benefits and procedures, since very few people take notes or remember details during interviews. Such written information, even if it consists of only one typed page, will help prevent the misunderstandings which occur when detailed information is passed on verbally.

Personnel should prepare a written interview schedule with the times and people (and their titles) the applicant will meet. This schedule should be included in the folder with a pad of paper. Both human nature and the delicate interaction that occurs in an interview process will discourage note taking, but the professional approach demands that the interviewer give the applicant that opportunity. Again, such a professional approach to interviewing—even though it requires minimal effort—should impress applicants and make them feel they have come to a "businesslike" and well-organized company.

Applicants from out of town require special consideration and preparation. A few years ago, before the shortage of experienced DP professionals, only middle- and upper-level managers relocated. But with the competition for experienced staff, some large organizations are now recruiting out-of-town project leaders, senior programmer/

analysts, and even entry-level programmers who have specialized talents or potential.

Although some companies have standard, well-planned hiring procedures for out-of-town employees which include relocation expenses and house-hunting trips, the "extras" may be missing and may contribute to a later morale and motivation problem. A company representative should meet the applicant at the airport, drive him or her to a motel, and present a packet with a local newspaper and assorted social, cultural, and sporting information. Anything that lets a person relate to a new community—even a map of the city—will increase the chance for a successful recruitment. The representative should treat out-of-town applicants as personal guests and show them the utmost in respect and consideration.

HOW DO YOU SCREEN APPLICANTS?

Every open position should be described by a set of qualifications regarding education, experience, and technical skills. Only rarely will a company find an applicant who will meet all those qualifications and have the right attitude toward the job. In the 1980s, with the shortage of trained, experienced professionals, the unanswered question in recruiting will be, "How far under the qualifications do we go?"

One answer is to look at the existing staff and study the background, qualifications, and attitudes of the more successful professional staff members. Does the applicant have anything in his or her background that compares to a current DP programmer or analyst? Perhaps the applicant came from the same educational program or worked in a local company known for its excellent practical experience. Perhaps the applicant has outside community interests similar to those of a staff member who is an energetic self-starter.

Unless the personnel department has a recruiter or director who is extremely knowledgeable in data processing, it is best to have all resumes sent to the hiring manager for screening. Occasionally, a potentially promising candidate is screened out by personnel and never seen by data processing. With the talent shortage of the 1980s few organizations can afford to overlook any potentially valuable employee.

INTERVIEWS SHOULD BE SMOOTH

The applicant should be met promptly and taken to the interviewer, who should give him or her the interview schedule and information packet. Letting an applicant wait even one minute past the appointed time is unexcusable. The first interviewer should phone ahead and verify that the second interviewer is available and waiting. Too often in a busy data processing shop, a manager or project leader is tied up in other meetings or in resolving production problems and simply not around when the personnel director brings in the applicant. This may be very common, but it still makes a bad impression.

It is also important to clean up the office used for interviews. Core dumps, program listings, stacks of reports spread over desks, and empty pizza cartons may be the norm in data processing, but they have no place in a formal interview. To insure the proper atmosphere, the interviewing manager should proceed as if the vice-president were dropping by for a meeting.

GETTING THE MOST INFORMATION

It is rare that an experienced DP professional can accurately size up the technical skills of an applicant and remember everything learned during the conversation. Too often, companies hire programmers and analysts and find weak areas that should have been pinpointed during the initial interview.

One good solution is to prepare a self-rating scale and checklist, which the applicant can use to list his or her specific hardware, software, and business experiences. The checklist can use a 1 to 5 rating scale for such skills as language or JCL, and a yes/no choice regarding familiarity with certain business skills or terms. The interviewer should tell the applicant that this form is merely a way to save time and help them both exchange information. Any written self-evaluation is also a good safeguard against applicants who may be tempted to misrepresent their abilities—people tend to be more careful when they put something in writing. The interviewer must stress that the evaluation form is only a tool to help both of them compare the applicant's background with the needs of the particular position. With the proper explanation, a written technical application should not create a threatening situation for the applicant.

The checklist should be subject to continuous review and will eventually evolve into a document that is tailored to an organization and its particular needs. It is unwise to spend too much time trying to develop a "perfect" rating scale and checklist on the first attempt.

Of course, any written material used during the initial interview must be carefully examined by the personnel department or even the legal department to insure that it does not violate federal and state discrimination statutes. Usually, however, a document that deals solely with technical matters will cause no problems.

MAKING A DECISION

Often the hardest part of the entire recruiting process in DP is deciding which applicant to hire and when. This decision can be made somewhat easier, and certainly more efficiently, if the company uses a standard post-interview decision procedure. Even in the larger, more organized companies, it is not uncommon to find managers who are so unsure about the next procedural step that the decision is delayed until one of the interviewers takes the initiative.

A decision plan should require a meeting of the interviewers within two business days of the interview. This is ample time for each manager to summarize and document on paper his or her reactions, conclusions, and recommendations about the applicant. The only possible recommendations are: (1) immediate hire; (2) immediate hire after a reference or background check; (3) not suitable; or (4) suitable if no better applicant found.

If the applicant is not qualified, or may be considered later, the personnel department or DP manager should immediately inform the applicant of this. The letter should be personal but clear and should not allow room for any doubt or misunderstanding. If the hiring manager wants to delay a decision pending other applicants, the letter should state as much and assure the applicant he or she will be informed if the position is filled. It is poor public relations to let applicants wonder where they stand and with the shortage of DP talent in the 1980s, it is important to maintain a positive professional reputation in the local DP community.

TRAINEES: TO HIRE OR NOT TO HIRE

DP managers often argue among themselves about the wisdom of recruiting trainees rather than experienced programmers or programmer/analysts. Trainees have the advantages of lower initial salary cost, higher availability, and a willingness to learn. The major disadvantage is that they are not immediately productive, except in the rare situation that the job requirements match a previous educational or learning experience. In most companies, however, DP executives believe that trainees will not be productive for at least a year.

Trainees are indeed a liability for at least six months—the amount of productive work produced by average trainees may not be worth their yearly salary and the cost of their training. From a strictly business viewpoint, the liability to the company is even greater when one adds the lost productive time of the senior trainer. Having said this much, one can ask: Are trainees in general worth considering for staff positions?

The answer is a qualified "yes." Hiring a trainee is justified if DP management considers the individual as a business investment and makes the decision based on a long-range consideration of their investment return.

Students just out of college are an excellent source of potential talent. Too often, managers are under pressure to fill open positions and hire a group of trainees whom they assume will somehow grow and become productive. But hiring trainees requires careful planning to establish a detailed, workable, training program for each new employee. A training program cannot be left to chance. Second-level DP managers report time and time again the familiar problem with trainees—after they stay a year and start to become productive, they suddenly leave, and the company loses most of its investment!

Senior DP management should not blame trainees for being "ungrateful." The actual problem lies in the training program. Too often, there just isn't any. Hiring trainees requires special considerations.

Specific requirements for a successful recruiting effort include:

1   Examine in detail the course work and level of sophistication of each trainee candidate.

A degree in computer science does mean a certain general knowledge of computer processing and methods, but experience has shown that computer science graduates, even from the same university, vary widely in their preparation for most business data processing positions. The student who has taken several business administration courses and who is proficient in COBOL is preferable to one who has concentrated upon compiler theory and design. Such knowledge about compiler operation may not be useful for someone who needs to work on an accounts payable system; likewise, a scientific programming position is not appropriate for a student who has taken heavy course work in economics and finance.

2   Don't place too much emphasis on grades.

Although grades are one common measurable goal of a college education, many DP managers now feel that grades themselves are only a very limited predictor of success in the business world.

3   Consider the personality of the candidate.

Success in most DP installations depends on positive interpersonal skills. Programming and systems analysis usually depends on interacting with user groups, the operations section, and other professionals. Trainees who appear to have difficulty relating to people during their interviews and in their college lives will not be the best candidates for a position that requires constant user interaction. Likewise, an extremely gregarious, talkative, and people-oriented college graduate may not be suitable for a position that involves individual effort and limited interaction with other people.

Of course, any personality judgment is basically subjective and must be integrated with the other factors that make up a final choice of candidates.

4   Notice the specific DP activities the applicant enjoys.

A computer science graduate who is "turned on" by large, complex, and tricky programming may not be the best programmer if the specific position calls for a simple, easily maintained code. Too often, university programs have not done a satisfactory job in preparing a student for practical job experience in the business data processing world, and the student and employer pay the price in terms of productivity and ease of maintenance. Those graduates who appear to look on data processing as a challenging game and get their satisfaction from using every complicated coding technique in the manual should be viewed with extreme caution.

5   Don't overestimate the skills of a new graduate.

Managers who assume a basic level of proficiency in JCL, programming, and systems understanding may be disappointed when hiring trainees. There is simply a limit to the skills a college computer science department can teach to students. Also, computer science as an educational field is still so new that business and scientific DP leaders have not had an adequate chance to provide universities with feedback on their results. It is better to underestimate rather than overestimate when hiring trainees.

6   Let the recruiting results determine the training plan.

Successful recruitment of DP personnel is only half the battle—DP management must develop a detailed, practical, and productive training plan for the new employees—both trainees and experienced professionals. Any new employee, from a $14,000 a year programmer trainee to a $25,000 a year senior programmer/analyst, requires training. Unfortunately, even in those companies which have highly professional and successful recruiting campaigns, training sometimes becomes almost a hit-or-miss proposition—with emphasis upon the miss.

The effects of not attaching a good training program to a successful recruiting effort are serious. First, since DP professionals tend to be more satisfied when they are productive and contributing toward the department, the new employees may become discouraged and develop a bad attitude. Second, and even worse, untrained employees are a losing investment for the organization. A manager who would recoil in horror at paying $20,000 a year for a machine that was not productive may accept without question a programmer/analyst who is not fully productive because he or she has not been trained. Proper training must follow the recruiting and hiring effort; with proper training, the time required for a new employee to become productive should drop dramatically. The people who manage the recruiting effort should either help with or manage the training program.

RECRUITING AND TRAINING

DP managers and senior staff should always consider the training effort that must match the recruiting campaign. Considerations of the training that will follow a successful recruiting effort may help in making the final recruiting and selection decisions.

The best way to start a sound training program is to appoint one experienced senior-level professional to serve as training coordinator and give him or her a set of guidelines. These guidelines are:

1   Examine in detail the requirements of the position.

Obviously, certain language skills, such as COBOL or Assembler, are necessary for a given position, but most jobs require a range of DP skills which may involve JCL, file design, system integration experience, familiarity with company organization and procedures, experience with dumps and debugging techniques, documentation experience, and computer operation knowledge. An excellent way to discover those specific skills is to ask the current staff for a daily and weekly job description—management may be very surprised by just what it actually takes to function successfully as a programmer or programmer/analyst.

2   Evaluate each new employee as an individual.

Both trainees and experienced DP professionals come to a company with a range of strengths and weaknesses, and the training director or supervisor cannot simply assume that employees know a subject simply because they say they do. OS JCL, for example, is a skill that ranges from knowing how to punch a correct job card to being able to design efficient JCL from a COBOL source listing.

The most efficient and accurate way to evaluate the employee is to create a detailed checklist of all of the skills needed to successfully do the particular job. A new programmer, for example, may need to understand step-level restarts in OS JCL, whereas a new systems analyst may need to know how to design reasonable edit requirements for general ledger input transactions.

This checklist would be similar to the one proposed for the initial screening and interview, but would be more detailed, and would be related to a specific job classification. With a realistic appraisal of each employee, the training coordinator should be able to develop a practical training plan which is not wasteful or redundant.

3   Find the best people for the training program.
Training is more difficult if one person is left with the entire job. A better approach is to select members of the professional staff to teach their particular areas of expertise. This not only widens the experience base of the new employees, but also introduces them to department members who can be of assistance in the future. This method also ensures that the training is more complete and the employee is exposed to more than one person's opinions and biases.

4   Design the training program from a top down approach.
Nothing is worse for new employees than to be plunged into the details of particular systems too quickly. The training coordinator needs to restrain the impulse to jump into details and skip over general matters. However, experience in training people indicates that the most successful training is usually built upon a firm general foundation of knowledge. The best training and education programs tend to proceed from a macro to a micro level. Also, giving new employees an understanding of the company or organization will tend to increase motivation and raise their morale.

SHOULD YOU HIRE PART-TIMERS?

An untapped source of labor is the increasing number of programmers and programmer/analysts who are looking for part-time, after-hours work, and the number of married professionals who want to spend some time with their families during the day but are willing to work at home or half-days at the office. In the 1970s, the typical management feeling was that only full-time employees were productive enough to be worth the money, but this attitude is quickly changing. More and more DP executives can point to specific success stories involving part-time employees, and even those who work at home. Using these professionals can be an excellent way to complete development or even documentation projects on time if the company cannot recruit or afford full-time staff members. Part-time programmers can often mean the difference between making and breaking a critical project deadline.

Recruiting such part-time talent is usually up to the individual company, since employment agencies rarely handle part-time work assignments. The best way to locate such people is to simply spread the word among the professional staff. Most employees who have been in data processing for several years have contacts in other organizations and companies. More than likely, someone will be recommended.

If word of mouth fails, a newspaper advertisement is the next step. The advertisement must be extremely specific as to language, operating system, and degree of system knowledge. It is not feasible, except in rare circumstances, to hire part-time, after hours employees and then train them in one or more specific skills. After hours programmers and those who work at home should be able to supervise and handle their own problems without detailed supervision.

A good procedure is to try a new programmer or analyst on a two-week trial basis—if things work out, he or she can be hired on a longer contract. The two-week arrangement allows the DP manager to gracefully terminate the arrangement if it does not prove satisfactory.

RECRUITING SHOULD NEVER STOP—ONLY SLOW DOWN

Even though a DP department may be fully staffed, DP and personnel department management must never forget recruiting. With turnover among programmers ranging between 10 to 50 percent a year, new openings are bound to occur at any time and management should be prepared. For example, if a programmer with excellent qualifications sends his resume to a company with no openings, a DP section or department manager should write back a short personal letter thanking the applicant for his or her interest. Unsolicited resumes and letters should never be ignored—they may be from people just right for the next unexpected job opening. Even people who are unqualified should never be totally ignored, since they may be better prepared in a year or two.

Obviously, responding positively to unsolicited applications is an excellent way to develop a positive, professional reputation in the local community.

FULFILLING EEO REQUIREMENTS

Many organizations—especially those with government contracts—must follow guidelines established by the Federal Equal Employment Opportunity provisions. The number of minority DP professionals is growing, but it is still small, and companies are competing among themselves to hire enough minority staff to satisfy those government requirements. Minority candidates can be more successfully recruited if company procedures and policies are somewhat modifed to make the positions and working environment more attractive. Of course, these policy changes will also help in recruiting and holding non-minority professionals.

Some specific actions are:

1.   Single parents (and married women with children) need to have an open phone line. Even if the professional staff has individual phone lines, management must still make sure that there is a reliable method for handling phone messages. A company without individual lines needs accessible phones for their employees to use on a reasonable basis. Although it is certainly possible for some employees to abuse phone privileges, adequate outside communication is still an excellent recruiting point.

2.   The use of "flextime" is increasing in large companies especially those located in the downtown or core city area. Having flexible hours does reduce traffic congestion and allows employees to modify their schedule to handle outside and family responsibilities. If a company does not have flextime, the data processing department can still authorize its supervisors to use discretion in handling those requests for occasional adjustments in hours. This flexibility is a strong attraction for women with children.

3.   Minority candidates may be attracted to companies and organizations that show some involvement in community and social affairs. This does not mean that a company should suddenly develop a community relations program solely as a method to help attract minority professionals. Such a program may fulfill an unspoken need for many people in the company, such as employees, stockholders, and senior management. People in general tend to feel more pride in their company if that organization is involved in their local community.

4.   Very large companies can organize special recruiting campaigns in colleges and universities with large minority populations, but most companies simply cannot afford that expense. One alternative is to make sure that current minority employees are aware of all job openings—this may lead to excellent results by word of mouth.

RECRUITING CAN BE SUCCESSFUL

Unfilled positions in data processing can ruin both development and maintenance project schedules and can even cause serious morale problems among the remaining staff. But if a company develops a professional and impressive recruiting plan, they will have the upper hand in the competition to hire DP talent in the 1980s.

6

Project and Task Management

Many books and articles on data processing management concentrate on large-scale development projects and present sophisticated, useful, and well-proven techniques for their control. After all, trying to manage the creation of a new sales reporting system is both complicated and exciting and soon becomes highly visible to everyone in the organization. Most DP installations, however, have far more actual labor allocated to smaller projects which involve production support, system maintenance, or minor system enhancements. These tasks may take only a few minutes or a few days, but DP managers who carefully analyze their labor costs will usually find that their largest system and programming expense is tied up in activities directly controlled not by middle or senior management, but by the project leader or even the individual programmers themselves! To a certain extent, this situation may be unavoidable in most business data processing organizations. But senior DP management should realize that this is an area where proper management direction and planning skills can simultaneously increase quality and reduce costs. A depart-

113

ment may not need all 15 highly paid professionals to support the current production systems if management is willing to critically examine the details of task control in the programming and systems section.

A frequent complaint from senior company management is that data processing people always appear to be busy, but DP managers cannot readily explain why the systems and programming staff cannot get to the high-paying or critical need projects. One reason is that the quality of small-project management is not as high as it could be and the programming staff is continually fighting to satisfy production support requirements and complete small requests which appear simple but actually eat up valuable professional resources. At the same time, project leaders and first-line supervisors report confusion at the prospect of managing those small but tricky tasks.

The solution is for middle and senior DP management to take the lead in solving this problem and provide the first-line supervisors with enough management direction to properly evaluate, document, assign, and subsequently monitor those small but frustrating production requirements.

PROPER EVALUATION COMES FIRST

Data processing requests can come from a wide range of sources, from the chairperson of the board to the part-time high school boy who helps decollate the multipart weekly sales report and almost everyone in between. In one sense, the diversity of input helps make data processing a dynamic, exciting profession, and it is also encouraging to see many people in the company making suggestions and requests and trying to utilize the computer as a tool to help them perform their own work. The time for DP management to worry is when users stop making requests! On the other side of the coin, however, is the confusion that can occur when all these verbal and written requests flood the data processing section without a smooth, documented, controlled, and businesslike system. Confusion inevitably results in low productivity and wasted professional time, much to the detriment of the DP department and the entire company.

All requests for DP services should come on a form specially designed for that purpose, and which may include a cover memo.

Requiring a written form not only discourages those casual, almost offhand requests that are apparently not worth the trouble of writing down, but also gives the evaluator a standard input mechanism with which to judge the value and complexity of the request. Too often a project leader or programming supervisor is handed a vague request that could either be a one-hour coding change or a total rewrite of an existing system and told to have a time estimate ready the next day at 8:00 A.M. In these situations, the evaluator is forced to define the original request, at least in terms of specific application systems, reports, and procedures and is, in effect, doing work that could possibly have been done by the submitter. A detailed form will force originators to consider aspects and definitions of the request they may not have thought about or even may not want to. The best management philosophy, as well as the current trend in data processing itself, is to involve the users in problem definition as well as in system design. A little informal education can do wonders for users who appear to need a system analyst or programming manager to help define a simple request. Although data processing is a service-oriented department, all actual and potential users have some responsibility to define their needs before formally involving data processing, and DP management has a responsibility to educate users so they can hold up their end of the partnership.

Companies which have allowed users to make requests verbally, by memo, or via the ever popular napkin from the company cafeteria, will find it difficult to ask users to start using a detailed request form. The objections will be reduced if DP management allows the users to help approve or even design the new form and if the formal announcement of the procedure includes the explanation that data processing is using the form to improve its service to the user departments or customers. Most users will accept such changes if they honestly believe that the new methods may improve service and help the data processing section meet their particular needs. In a few rare cases, a DP manager may need to apply pressure through company management to force certain reluctant users to follow the new procedure. Although this eventually works, it should only be used as a last resort since it will alienate the user and may cause serious political repercussions in the future.

The form should identify the requestor, his or her need, a priority ranking for the change or addition, and enough basic detail so a programmer/analyst can understand the complexity of the proposed task. The style and format of a good form is not important as long as it provides the programmer with enough basic information for him or her to efficiently evaluate, channel, and set priorities for the requests. Comments should be placed at several locations on the form to demonstrate that data processing is concerned about the "cost" of the proposed change in terms of labor, computer development time, and ongoing computer resources. Even if the department has no chargeback facility for in-house users or outside customers, a strong emphasis on cost must start on the request form itself and become virtually automatic to both users and data processing people. Nothing in this world is free, and that includes application system changes or enhancements, new systems, and computer resources. Users, customers, and data processing staff members become more valuable employees to the company when they understand that fact of life. This is one area where managers can begin to produce programmers, programmer/analysts, systems analysts, and paraprofessionals who are fully productive employees from a company-wide business viewpoint. When this happens, the data processing organization will finally start on the road to maturity. Too often DP staff members—including managers—fail to understand the vast economic value of their efforts and personnel allocations. The data processing section appears to outsiders to be a collection of technical wizards who dash madly from project to problem and play with the hardware and software as if it were their hobby. Interestingly enough, outsiders have a habit of being right!

Every request should receive a preliminary evaluation by the next working day. The evaluator needs to examine the request and determine whether the form has enough information for a correct evaluation or needs additional definition from the user or a systems-analyst/user meeting. A one-line change to a program or simple system change can be scheduled immediately, whereas more complex requests will be analyzed according to a priority assignment determined by the management team.

The correct priority of any request is, quite frankly, almost as hard to evaluate as the request itself. Customer and users differ in their sensitivity to data processing schedules and commitments. The personal relationship between the submitter and the evaluator also plays a part. Of course, a request from senior company management may in effect become a demand rather than a request, and the DP manager or MIS director must tactfully examine the request and its implications before committing valuable resources.

The first action performed on any request should be an evaluation of its practicality in the current data processing environment. A request to print in red any stock item that has a negative balance should be returned out of hand to the user with an explanation that most line printers only print in one color. A request to print a copy of the Monday morning weekly sales report on Friday should be returned with a note tactfully explaining that the Monday morning analysis can only be created after the Saturday sales are processed. A user who requests major additions to the accounts receivable master file should be told that such additions constitute a major project request, and that he or she already has seven other projects waiting on the accounting department priority list.

If the request is practical and reasonable, it should be evaluated for immediate action. A significant number of data processing tasks are standard and fairly straightforward requests that are either required for production support purposes or are so simple that it is easier to make the change than to explain to the user why it cannot be done. In virtually all cases, since data processing is correctly classified as a service organization, the user or customer should get the benefit of the doubt.

Occasionally, a customer or client may continually abuse his or her data processing privileges and request unjustifiable changes or modifications. Another problem occurs when, out of curiosity, a user wants detailed explanations of an error or unusual situation. It is inappropriate to tell customers that they are abusing the facilities and that no one really cares what happens when the budget load transaction has only three periods of data instead of the twelve periods required by both the system and the documentation. If the edit system informed the user of the error and how to correct it, data processing has done its job. The better solution is to work with the clients and try to make them more cost conscious—every investigation, research, or test costs the company money and should have at least minimal justification. The same answer should be given to the requestor who asks that the date field be moved one space to the left and the page number placed on the bottom line instead of the top—the time and effort involved may not be justified from a total company standpoint.

Getting this important message across may require tactful interaction between senior DP management and the users. It is better to inform clients that their requests will not be honored than to put the requests on a schedule knowing full well that they will never be completed. This approach of "put it on the list and forget it" is very common in most DP shops because the first-line supervisors who evaluate these requests are reluctant to offend user managers. It is the responsibility of DP second- and third-level management to uncover these situations, determine if it is expedient to work with the user, and follow through with tactful suggestions and education. Saying no to users who are either purposely or inadvertently eating up large chunks of DP resources is not easy, but management has never been easy. Experience indicates that most users will respect managers who are honest with them, as long as the honesty is tempered with fairness and understanding.

MANAGING REQUESTS

If the request is justified, the project leader, systems analyst, or programming manager should assign it a priority by considering the timing of the request, the educational value to the person doing the task, and the current and future workload of the section. Whatever the priority, it should be placed on a numbered list which gives everyone some idea as to when it will be done.

Managing a list of small projects is in some ways more difficult than controlling a formalized project with well-defined checkpoints and written specifications. The goal should not be simply to pass out assignments according to priority sequence, but to effectively manage the programming and systems resource so the maximum work can be done in the minimum time.

One technique is to arrange the priority list so that tasks with a low priority automatically have their value raised by the passage of time. That is, a very low priority project that has been waiting for six months should be raised in priority so it eventually comes to the top of the list and gets its chance. Six months, or perhaps a year, is the longest permissible time for a task to remain on a list—after that much waiting time it should either be completed or dropped from the list with a frank explanation to the user who requested the task. A management team that follows the "egoless management" philosophy will not be overly concerned with its image, and the individual managers and section leaders will find it easier to be honest with the people they are serving. If the data processing section cannot get a request done because of other commitments, it is far better to face that fact openly. Businesses in the 1980s have far too much to accomplish to allow their employees the luxury of playing games with each other.

A second method is to group tasks in such a way that changes to modules, programs, and even systems can be performed at one time, in order to save both personnel and machine resources. Such combined projects are usually more interesting to a programmer or programmer/analyst than a single one-line programming change. Also, it is usually more efficient to compile, link, and test a module with several changes than to test it one change at a time.

A third way to properly manage tasks is to determine which ones can be done by paraprofessionals or clerks. Submitting a routine job, for example, can usually be done by a clerk or trained paraprofessional just as well as by a programmer. With proper instruction and supporting documentation, nonprofessionals can complete the small projects and tasks formerly done by a programmer, especially in the area of production support, system maintenance, and administrative support. Managers, especially first-line supervisors, need to continually analyze their workload of small projects and tasks to find ways to increase productivity.

Another method to properly manage small projects is to consider automating some of the periodic but routine requests. For example, updating a table of report requests can perhaps be done on a calendar set up by division and department. The weekly and monthly report numbers would be assigned to each reporting date and maintained by a clerk in the sales department. Hard-coded logic to perform a cost recalculation on a master file by customer number can be replaced by generalized logic and a switch that can be set by the customer himself.

Of course, the first-level manager should always consider the cost of automating the task and the savings in terms of time and increased productivity. A pay-off in time alone is only half of the justification for replacing manual procedures with an automatic technique because the reduced chance for error and the increased programmer availability may be even more significant. That is, a task that takes a programmer 30 minutes a week may take only 30 minutes during the week, but that time does not count the "mental interruption" to the individual. The programmer must change his or her mental set and regain the orientation to the major project or original tasks when that 30-minute task is done. If the calculated break-even point on automating a particular function is two years, it may not seem worthwhile until the manager considers the number of errors caused by the manual procedure and the interruption to a programmer's important project development time.

The fifth technique to increase productivity is to evaluate the time required for requests that have been completed on both a regular and intermittent basis. One would expect that a request will take less effort the second time around. If this is not the case, the request is either being accomplished in the shortest time possible, or the programmers (or other employees) have not properly learned the procedure. Programmers and systems analysts frequently report that it often takes them more time to determine how to accomplish a given task than to actually do the work. Looking at this situation from a logical viewpoint, it is reasonable to expect that, once the data processing department has completed a request, the technique or method should become established. *In most DP shops this transfer of knowledge simply does not happen!*

It is the responsibility of management to verify that the information learned by the first staff member who successfully handled the assignment is passed on to other staff members who will eventually have responsibility for those same tasks. Information about job assignments is, after all, the property of the company and does not truly belong to the individual who spent company time learning that information. The best way to guarantee such a transfer of knowledge is to require that every routine or standard request in the shop be documented and available to all staff members. Such documentation can even be used in a formalized training program, especially in production support environments where a programmer or analyst will be expected to spend at least some time performing these tasks or other assignments which may resemble the task.

The original programmer should include in the documentation any control streams or jobs used to complete the task. The staff should feel a professional obligation to pave the way for the next employee who must complete that same task—in this manner the time required to process those requests will decrease and spur a corresponding increase in productivity.

A final technique in managing small projects and tasks is to search first for other methods to accomplish the same goal. In some instances, a user may make a request that could be better handled by a minor adjustment in the user's operating procedures than by a programming and systems modification. For example, an accounts receivable manager may ask for a list of accounts sorted by zip code, when he could use a copy of the mailing label list that is already in that sequence. Often a good systems analyst or programmer familiar with the business application and the user's operating procedures can propose alternate methods to solve a business data processing need. The method may be a new use for an old report, an extra copy of a report listing, a change in the customer's work schedule, or a manual procedure that will take 10 minutes a week but will accomplish the same goal as a 30-minute special computer run costing two hours of programmer set-up time. All first-line supervisors who evaluate work requests should constantly look for alternate noncomputer solutions and should never assume that everything in the world must be done by computer. Some things are simply not right for computer processing.

ASSIGNMENT IS A SKILL

The easy way to assign small projects is simply to pass them out to the staff and give each programmer or analyst a deadline. This approach, of course, could be handled just as well by the data processing secretary as an expensive project leader! However, assigning the right task to the right individual is an excellent opportunity to help develop a better-trained professional staff, and to increase productivity by allowing the staff to feel some degree of control over their environment. People in general work harder when they feel some responsibility for their projects and tasks.

One obvious rule is to avoid repeatedly giving the same type of assignment to the same person. This pattern leads quickly to a bored, frustrated, and eventually careless professional. From the programmer's viewpoint, routine jobs lose their attraction and interest after a while, and the professional begins to feel like part of a factory assembly line. Although some DP executives believe this style makes the programmers more motivated and confident, the opposite is usually the case. Productivity will drop when a programmer/analyst believes that he or she is destined to perform inventory file reorganizations for the rest of his or her natural life. Very rarely will any professional be satisfied with a routine, highly predictable job situation.

A more productive management style is to vary assignments so the staff can continually look forward to at least slight variations in daily routine. This may not always be possible in a shop which has a large number of routine projects, but the project leader or first-line supervisor should always consider varying the job assignments to help keep the staff motivated. A second benefit is that by continually changing assignments the professional staff will train each other, a very valuable benefit when the DP manager suddenly finds her sales reporting system expert is leaving in two weeks. The cross-training principle alone is enough justification to spread the work assignments so that each programmer and analyst gets at least a brief experience in more than one application system or production area.

Contrary to popular opinion, a first-line supervisor can successfully allow the experienced professional to help him or her schedule and assign most project requests. It is not a matter of a project leader giving up some authority, but rather a policy that allows employees to see the entire load of work requests and to offer their own opinions on proper allocation. Having at least some control over their workload may increase morale and produce more motivated employees who can better understand the pressures and responsibilities of a data processing unit. Too often a professional will have no realistic idea of the work backlog and the vast number of people who demand changes and improvements to the production systems. A programming team which understands these facts may be more motivated and more productive.

THE DOUBLE "M's"—MONITORING AND MOTIVATION

Every professional in data processing needs to have all available pertinent information before starting a task, but too often a first-line supervisor will give the employee only the information he or she thinks the programmer needs. This frequently results in a communication chasm, rather than a mere communication gap, and the employee suffers from incomplete facts, misunderstanding, and bad assumptions which can be corrected only by frequent sessions with the supervisor. Whereas it is theoretically possible for a manager to consistently give staff members too much unnecessary information, opinions, and facts about a task, this style is rare in data processing. The "egoless management" philosophy requires that employees be given information freely so they can learn to separate the important from the unimportant and develop additional knowledge about the task, their job, and the company. A first-line manager who hands his or her staff a work order with the standard two-word instruction "Do it" is missing the major thrust of the position and badly needs management instruction. If a middle manager observes that programmers, system analysts, and other staff people must regularly consult with their immediate supervisor on assigned tasks, it is highly possible that the supervisor did not understand the assignment properly, the employee has not yet been trained adequately, or the supervisor did not do a satisfactory job explaining the work requirements to the employee. This third situation needs to be corrected quickly for the sake of the department, the employees, and the supervisor.

Assuming the programmer or other professional has been given satisfactory information on the requirements of the task, the supervisor or manager must then determine the best way to monitor the progress of the assignment. It is interesting to note that the true purpose of a supervisor is not to directly control the progress of the staff, but rather to manage the environment so the employees can become fully productive. The best way, therefore, to monitor small- or even medium-level assignments is to spend as much effort investigating the reasons for the current status as on investigating the exact details of every file layout, program module, and test in progress. A manager who spends an hour going over the exact blow-by-blow, line-by-line status of an assignment will have most likely wasted that entire hour, unless the staff member is so new that he or she needs such detailed help. Rather, the supervisor should spend at least half that time trying to uncover reasons for the surprising progress or lack of progress.

If an individual is adequately trained and prepared, and if the time estimate for the task was reasonable, the supervisor needs to discover the "why" and "how" of any unusual situation. Problems just don't happen in data processing. They happen for reasons which need to be analyzed by at least the first-level manager and probably his or her superior. An equally possible situation—although far less frequent—is that a programmer may suddenly forge ahead on a task and complete three weeks of checkpoints in one week. After the manager has congratulated the staff member and let him or her bask in that rare glory of a project done ahead of schedule, the manager's next step is to discover why that task was completed in so short a time. Successes in data processing do not happen any more than problems just happen, and both conditions need to be fully analyzed—the "problems" so they can be reduced and the "successes" so they can be increased. Perhaps the original time estimate was wrong, or the employee may have discovered ways to speed up the project. Whatever the reason, it is the job of the manager to ask the question "Why?" until he or she finds those reasons. Sometimes the reasons for delays are beyond the control of the programming and systems group, but they still need to be carefully documented and discussed with senior management.

Along with the core dump, personal friction between operators and programmers, and the Friday night trips to the local place of good cheer, the weekly report is a tradition in data processing and is the most common of the formal reporting methods. Many installations, especially those involved in extensive production support work, use the weekly report to monitor the status of small projects and tasks. This can be useful if management is willing to upgrade the weekly report form so that it accurately reports not only a single employee's week on the job, but also the management's overall view of all performance. In other words, a simple description of the current status of a programmer's or system analyst's project on Monday morning is nothing more than a snapshot and is typical of most weekly project and task-reporting forms. With proper analysis and thought, however, it can be turned into a meaningful tool to help create a well-managed section and boost departmental productivity.

A good weekly reporting procedure must consider the nature of the tasks being reported. A programmer or system analyst assigned many small tasks should use a different form than a programmer engaged in formal project work with definite planned milestones. It is a mistake to believe that only one "super form" can handle all week-ly or monthly reporting requirements.

For small tasks that take a week or less in calendar time, the week-ly reporting form should include a line for every task in progress and an identification number that refers to a master log of requests on the department's priority list. Next to the log number should be a space for a short, descriptive name of the task, and next to that should be the name of the requesting unit or person. It is important that professional staff at all levels know who has requested the job. This will do wonders in helping to "humanize" the high-pressure data processing environment.

Next to the requesting unit or person should be four columns which correspond to the four cycles of almost all small projects—*evaluation, in-progress, completed,* and *follow-up.* A checkmark under the proper heading will immediately reveal the general status of the task.

Four dates should be on the form for each task: the date the proj-ect or task was assigned, the date the programmer began work on the task, the estimated completion date, and the actual completion date. Next to the actual completion date should be a column to indicate time-critical assignments that have been promised by DP manage-ment. Payroll tax changes, for example, are usually time-critical assignments. The last space should be reserved for a summary of the task and any comments the staff member believes are pertinent.

The form should include specific sections for noting general problems, suggestions concerning the work environment, and a sum-mary of the entire week. These sections can be just as valuable as those dealing with specific tasks. A manager's job is not only to monitor the progress of assignments, but also to analyze the condi-tions that determine that progress or lack of progress. Employees in data processing should also be taught to look beyond the traditional report that "The accounts payable fix is half done, but I am still having trouble testing it" or "The new general ledger tran code edit worked fine, but the new program accidentally rejected every other transaction code and the accounting manager is threatening to push me in the paper shredder."

The free-form sections of the weekly report can be used to explain the "why's" of each situation. Can the programmer explain why it is taking him so long to test the accounts payable fix? Is there someone else in the shop who has tested AP5043 and had a test deck already prepared? Did he schedule a specific test time with operations, or is he using the entire accounts payable update when only one department's data would be enough for a valid parallel? Why did the general ledger edit change cause all those errors? Did the analyst understand the logic of the system before designing the change requirements? In other words, do we really want to accept the high turnover in data processing caused by losing programmers to the paper shredder? What could be done next time to prevent another angry user?

Knowing the status of each task is only half the battle—managers must also train themselves and their staffs to analyze the situation and develop ways to improve performance. Data processing projects do not proceed evenly, but rather, involve a complex and integrated human/machine interaction which flows at various rates. In most cases, the smarter the worker and the smarter the working habits, the faster the tasks will get done. The order of magnitude is not just a few percent, but may be several thousand percent!

The last required section should include the plans of the employee for the next week or reporting period. The best time to plan ahead is right after one has summarized the past week's activities and analyzed one's own performance. Data processing professionals tend to work independently, and as independent workers, they should never be allowed to come into a new week or new reporting period without having a realistic, written set of objectives. They may be called "goals," "planned accomplishments," or "objectives," but every DP staff member needs his or her own set before starting work. Observation of programmers, programmer/analysts, and system analysts, indicates that the best performers tend to be those who plan their work before they start. This valuable skill should be taught to all DP staff people.

A very useful addition to any reporting form is a time and cost breakdown. For internal purposes, in the 1980s, a DP manager can easily justify an estimate of 35 dollars per hour of professional time, which would include salary, fringe benefits, and supporting requirements. A task which takes six hours, such as modifying and testing a new sort sequence in the payroll reporting stream, does indeed cost the company $210, and the employee who must calculate his or her own value to the organization may suddenly realize the importance of his or her personal time-management abilities. Supervisors can tell a programmer or analyst how valuable his or her time is, but there is no substitute for showing that value in dollars and cents. People understand money better than they understand hours. Time and cost breakdown are the start of a good internal or external charge-back system, and they can be justified solely on the basis of their motivational value.

Another way to increase motivation is to allow the person completing the assignment to notify the requesting unit or person that the fix or change has been made. In too many shops the DP manager or project leader will automatically reserve this satisfying duty for himself. If the management team is practicing "egoless management," the professional and paraprofessional staff get the ego boost and subsequent motivational charge by following their projects through to the end and playing the "hero" role.

All tasks should be assigned a control or log number as soon as it is accepted. If the project leader or systems analyst pays careful attention to the format of the log number, it can pay dividends when managers want to analyze the nature of requests and small projects. A sequential log number, such as R462, is better than saying "Change department 10 edit in the payroll system" every time someone refers to that request, but it gives no other important information. Enlarging the control or log number slightly will give much more information and will allow some basic analysis of the workload. For example, if the information systems division services nine departments, including accounting, finance, and sales, a two-character prefix for each request, followed by a sequential control number, would be appropriate. A code of "R" for research or "F" for fix will provide further information regarding the request. The application system, such as order entry, or shop control, can also be made part of the control log number. If a log number or code is too long and confusing to be practical, the analyst can devise a short code having only requesting division, sequential number, and an additional suffix that is tacked on when the request is first evaluated. For example, "FIN119" may refer to request number 119 which was made by the financial section, but the formal task identification should be "FIN119-APF," which more accurately describes a fix to the accounts payable system. A simple computer program can sort the requests or projects and print very interesting analyses. Often a decision to create a meaningful log number will lead to the eventual design of a true time-accounting system that is molded to the particular needs of a data processing department.

WHEN IS "DONE" REALLY "DONE"?

Every DP supervisor or manager has complained that programmers, programmer/analysts, and system analysts sometimes fail to finish a task. The programmer may have spent 17 hours setting up the special year-end payroll run and triple-checked every detail and then forgot to tell the operations manager it was ready. Or, the system analyst may have finished the intricate and sophisticated design interface between the minicomputers in Boston and the mainframe in Los Angeles but failed to realize that with a 1200-baud line, the daily transmission would take 35 hours a day. The new budget transaction code addition may have been implemented in record time but unfortunately updated last year's figures rather than the current year's. These mistakes may be very common, but they can be prevented by teaching professionals the importance of follow-up. Despite the pleas and exhortations of frustrated managers, data processing personnel will always make some mistakes, especially in those small tasks and assignments in both maintenance and development work which have few well-defined checkpoints. Successful managers, however, can usually train a professional staff to catch most of those errors themselves.

The technique is to teach programmers, analysts, and all other staff members who are engaged in various levels of intellectual work to "step back," examine their work, and look for errors. This is contrary to the typical human reaction, which is to praise oneself when a task is completed and feel positive about the results of the project. People will and should feel good about their accomplishments, but an accomplished, productive DP professional must have the ability to critically examine his or her own results and find mistakes that do not appear on the surface.

To a certain extent this ability requires an individual to temporarily push aside "ego" and look at his or her work without letting pride interfere with judgments or decisions. One might call this "egoless self management" and is possible only in those environments where managers and directors tend to practice "egoless management" and demonstrate to their employees that they can realistically evaluate their own results and job performance.

In a DP shop where the style is to manage upwards or to play excessive politics with management-level decisions, it is doubtful if the data processing staff can be effectively taught to critically examine their own positions, results, and completed work. People, after all, tend to follow the example of their superiors, and if they see managers who are excessively concerned with their own public image, they will usually acquire some of the same tendencies and will be unable to accurately examine themselves and their work.

Looking for errors can take many forms, but the specific type of errors found in most data processing installations are remarkably similar and are related to the nature of the task.

Programming changes are particularly liable to mistakes, and the programmer or programmer/analyst who designs and codes the modification should ask himself these questions:

1 Does the coding change exactly match the request?
2 Does the request appear reasonable, and does the user really want what is down on paper?
3 What are the possible effects or potential problems that can be caused by this change?
4 Should any other coding changes be done at the same time, either to that module or to any related programs?
5 Who else should know about the change? Do operations, the documentation specialist, or the other programming sections care or need to know that a module is being changed? Will they find out the hard way?
6 Were there any assumptions made in the original request which may be invalid, incorrect, or incomplete?
7 When should the user be told that the change is in production? Does he or she need advance warning?

Although most programming for small tasks is done individually,

DP managers should insist that another programmer or analyst briefly look at a change ready to go into production. If the data processing management team is indeed practicing "egoless management," the professional staff will be able to practice "egoless programming" and allow others to check their work without feeling threatened or insulted. It is not a matter of lacking trust in people, but simply a very helpful procedure to require another professional evaluation before a change becomes permanent. Perhaps if another programmer had looked at the new general ledger tran code edit change, he or she might have caught the logic error that rejected all transaction codes except one and spared the original programmer the severe physical pain of the paper shredder. Another look at the material by a peer can do wonders by helping catch obvious mistakes before they affect production and damage user confidence.

Such a team approach can be successful if the staff puts aside their natural feelings of pride and "personal ownership" of the work. It may be necessary for an "egoless manager" to carefully explain the logic and benefits behind the team approach.

Operational tasks are almost as error prone as programming changes. Some typical questions are:

1   Was this special procedure performed correctly according to the instructions?
2   Were the instructions reasonable?
3   Has the output been given to the right person and identified as a special run?
4   Was there any required balance procedure?
5   Who should be notified that the operational task is complete?
6   Can this cause related problems, and can those problems be prevented?

Research or investigative tasks are very common in most business data processing installations, and the person doing the research should ask himself questions such as:

1   Does the answer give the requestor what he or she needs?
2   How sure am I about the answer?

3   Was there a better way to find the answer or solve the problem? Could documentation have solved the problem sooner? Would other techniques have given the same answer?

SUMMARY

Good managers cannot assume that because small tasks and individual projects are so common in business data processing everyone who handles such assignments automatically knows the most efficient way to handle them. Rather, observation shows that the opposite situation is more often true. Many senior professionals and first-line supervisors follow only one method or style of managing their own tasks and those of people who report to them, but their particular method has never been analyzed for efficiency and productivity. The classic description of a data processing department that is always busy "fighting fires" or trying to satisfy users is one indication that the procedures for handling small projects must be analyzed and improved.

7

Quality Control:
The Missing Link

Take a group of experienced programmers or systems analysts and lock them in a room with 200 angry, frustrated users. Tell them you have a very important question and the answer must be 100 percent honest or they will never leave the room. The question is simply, "Of all the projects and systems in data processing you have been involved with or seen, what percentage has been work that you would call 'high quality'?" If that group of professionals is honest and is typical of most veteran data processing employees, the answer will range from about 20 percent to zero. Quality has never been a strong point in either the business or scientific data processing community.

The signs of this lack of quality are all around us. Although they may be unpleasant and mildly annoying, these indications must be understood by a majority of DP managers and senior professionals if data processing management is ever to assume its rightful place as the equal of other management teams in the organization.

One frequently overlooked indicator is the usually unspoken frustration felt by both managers and staff personnel when they finish a major project, or even their everyday duties. Many staff members, especially those who have worked in several installations, consistently feel unsure about their performance and the quality of the application systems they produce or maintain. The frequent complaint, "It's impossible to do a good job here" is based on a feeling of frustration; even six- and seven-day work-weeks seldom solve the entire problem. Some projects are late or even cancelled entirely. Maintenance requests are often a nightmare and cause more problems than they solve. New hardware and software designed to improve processing and provide exciting challenges seem to have only partial success. Many data processing employees never seem to be proud of their accomplishments.

Another sign of "lack of quality" is the external management concern with the detailed operational aspects of data processing. Other areas of the company are usually managed at a high level, and the senior executive staff allows divisions such as accounting and marketing to run their own sections and interferes only when cross-division problems arise or some policy decision must be made. In the world of data processing, however, most senior executives simply do not trust the DP management team as much as they trust the inventory control managers or the budget planning executives. This feeling may be in part due to the mystique that unfortunately still surrounds the computer, but it is more likely due to past errors, omissions, and plain, old-fashioned poor performance. Obviously, a DP department in some lucky companies had the right combination of people, users, hardware, and software to put together a set of application systems that everyone in the company can be proud of, but this is definitely the exception rather than the rule. Some software development companies which develop and market commercial application packages have recently taken the lead in quality control and are now marketing extremely well-designed, well-implemented, and thoroughly documented systems. In the 1980s, senior company management will still harbor the same unspoken reservations about DP managers and their staff they had during the 1970s. Those concerns are too often based upon real events.

If user satisfaction is any indicator of the quality of the entire profession, then high-quality systems must be few and far between. The extremely fast marketing success of the distributed data processing hardware vendors points not only to an age when DDP is practical, but to a long-term frustration felt by users at all levels. Managers among nontechnical users are ready and willing to buy their own hardware and software because they feel data processing is not responsive to their needs.

THE CRISIS OF QUALITY

The manufacturing industry learned long ago that, because of the speed and complexity of the assembly line, it was necessary to create a separate quality control department which reported directly to senior management and functioned as a "quality assurance" group. Such a section guaranteed that the output of the company was complete and timely and met accepted standards. The line managers themselves were not given this direct responsibility, since they were too involved with running their own departments. Although senior management sometimes restricted the power of a quality-control team, and thereby reduced its effectiveness, the concept was well-proven in many industries: by giving more authority to the quality-control group, the organization could produce better finished merchandise. Total production would usually decrease temporarily, but everyone involved—from the workers on the assembly line to the president of the company to the customer who bought the product—would be satisfied with the final output. The theory worked well in practice, as shown by the successful redirection of the Japanese industrial effort in the 1970s.

If data processing is indeed in a "crisis of quality," the only logical answer is to copy the principle of the deliberate separation of the quality-control function from line management. The programming managers and project leaders can still be responsible for the management direction and supervision of their various sections, but the quality-control concept demands that a separate individual or group monitor the quality of data processing. The environment of a typical management information systems division is now as complicated as a manufacturing assembly line, and it is unrealistic to expect the line managers to faithfully and consistently monitor the quality of such abstract products as programming and systems analysis. Top-quality work seldom appeared in the 1960s or 1970s and is even less likely to appear in the even more complex decade of the 1980s.

A lack of concern for quality is not new to data processing, and it is possible that three of the historical factors which contributed to this state of affairs are still operating in some installations: a preoccupation with deadlines, an overemphasis on complexity as opposed to simplicity, and a career path that ignores the importance of quality programming.

Deadlines are an accepted fact of life in the business world and cannot be ignored, but in too many situations senior company management has focused so much on meeting an artificial deadline that they have forced systems into production before they were ready. The DP manager may have looked successful, but from a true management perspective his or her management of that system may have been a failure if the application was not developed in a high-quality manner and will require extensive follow-up and correction. Too few data processing executives had the courage to postpone a project long enough to do a quality job, and too few senior executives realized the problems they were causing by trying to stick fanatically to a deadline that was made before the project was even defined. A lack of quality can unfortunately be traced to management direction.

DP management has not stressed quality programming and has usually been more interested in meeting user-imposed deadlines than in turning out quality systems and programming. Managers and directors have ignored the often-mentioned but seldom-followed rule that bad programming always catches up with the company, and it costs more to maintain a poorly-designed system than it would have cost to do a quality job for the first time around. Too often, corporate management has not seen the dollars and cents justification for trying to create professional, high-quality systems, perhaps because DP managers have never really proved to themselves that it is in the company's best interest to turn out a good "product."

The data processing profession has not stressed such basic essentials as logical and simple program design, meaningful variable names, common structures for all programs to use, comments and internal documentation, and simple, straight-forward programming. The recent emphasis on structured and top-down programming is an indication that the DP profession is becoming concerned with program quality, but a new programming style is only part of the solution. Changing to a structured or top-down approach may help in some cases, but it is entirely possible to still wind up with programs and systems that are hard to follow, hard to understand, poorly documented, and almost impossible to change.

The career path in data processing in general, and specifically in most business DP departments, does not usually encourage quality programming and system design. Even though programs are the final product of a programming section, the trainees and less-experienced programmers are usually given the program design and coding assignments. The more experienced programmers and programmer/analysts tend to move away from such tasks. The trend continues to the first-level supervisor, usually a project leader, who proudly announces to the world that he or she is now away from coding and is doing more "important" work.

Unfortunately, this belief that the true professional should move away from coding and into more "interesting" work ignores the fact that coding and program design are just as important to the data processing world as the system design itself. A poorly written system can be a financial curse to a company, in terms of maintenance costs, programmer morale, and user satisfaction.

Programming is simply too important to be left solely to trainees, or to the programmer who thinks of a program as personal property. Any production program should represent the best effort of the entire programming section, and both peer review and peer pressure should be used to enforce quality programming standards.

Data processing departments must change their philosophy and provide a career path for programmers who show talent and a desire to remain programmers. A good programmer or program designer is simply too valuable to move into another position just because of salary or status considerations. Actually, an experienced programmer who can consistently and quickly turn out high-quality programs should be on the same status and salary level as a first-line supervisor. Entry-level programmers should be shown a career path that emphasizes programming as a skill and reaffirms the importance of high-quality programs and application systems.

DECISIONS, DECISIONS

The decade of the 1980s will reveal a serious problem in the area of *technological quality,* indicated by incorrect decisions on major hardware and software issues. In the late 1970s, when minicomputers finally proved their cost effectiveness and reliability, many DP management teams were forced to choose almost blindly between the centralized and distributed approaches to business system design questions. Some chose the centralized approach because it had been proven successful in many previous situations, while other companies selected the distributed approach because it was new and obviously showed great promise. Few managers, however, made those critical decisions based on hard facts rather than emotion and personal prejudices, and the quality of those important business decisions was often poor. Technological choices are rarely right or wrong; rather, their quality is measured by the lasting suitability of that choice over a period of months or even years. The quality of such decisions and commitments is dependent not only on the skill and experience level of the senior staff, but also on the facts the team has to work with. Obviously, hardware and software choices will often help set the standard for the quality of the data processing section and possibly even the entire organization. Poor quality decisions and choices up front usually mean low-quality application systems and unacceptable service to the users, who are ultimately paying for the data processing solution to their business needs.

The solution to the technological quality problem is twofold. First, the educational and skill level of the decision makers must be raised, and, second, these people must be required to gather enough facts to make a sound business decision. One advantage to the "egoless management" philosophy is that managers can treat decision making as a skill to be devloped rather than assuming that a good manager instinctively knows how to make the correct choices.

Managers and senior professionals who are put in decision making roles come with individual backgrounds and qualifications. A manager who must evaluate a distributed data processing approach to claims payment for an insurance company either has previous distributed experience or does not. In many situations during the 1980s, it will not be possible to find people experienced with new technology to make those complicated technological choices—the company may have no one employed who can utilize direct experience to help make high-quality decisions when they are needed. Even consultants may not be a realistic alternative if they are too expensive. One example is a company considering the use of fiber optics to implement a new high-volume communication network between two buildings—very few people have first-hand experience with fiber optics. Although it is always possible to locate and hire consultants to help with certain critical problem areas, companies will still find other decisions that can only be made by the internal staff.

The answer to this frustrating situation is to encourage the management and senior staff to engage in self-education by reading trade journals and newspapers to keep current with new technological developments. Indeed, such extracurricular reading should be a requirement for those who must make recommendations regarding software, hardware, and application designs. Formal seminars led by experts in topics of direct concern to a specific project are valuable in many individual situations, but managers or executives will not be ready to understand the details of any given subject unless they have tried to keep themselves in step with the general direction of data processing.

The second answer to the technological quality control problem is to admit that high-quality business decisions cannot be made without gathering, digesting, and analyzing facts as opposed to wishy-washy discussions based upon the verbal presentation skill of a salesperson or the size of the free lunch courtesy of the last marketing representative. The fact-gathering process begins and ends with formal written documents. A plan to install a minicomputer system in a warehouse must start with a list of specifications of the purpose and planned value of the entire system, with detailed functional specifications as to input, output, and processing features. The time to talk with salespeople and read detailed product literature is after the system requirements have been defined. Persuasive literature has been known to influence many technological decisions, with disappointing results.

One of the best but seldom used tricks in gathering facts is to contact organizations that have either studied the same general issues or who have actually selected one of the options being considered. Any legitimate hardware or software vendor should be willing to provide references who are willing to share their experiences with a particular data base or computer system. Obviously, the vendor will never knowingly suggest someone who has a definitely unfavorable attitude toward his or her product or service, but some probing questions can often uncover significant problems and potential drawbacks that will never be mentioned by a marketing representative. Often, a current user can mention other installations which have had less-favorable experiences with the product in question.

Once the management or senior staff has defined the requirements as precisely as it can and has researched both the general topic and the specific alternatives, it is time to evaluate the choices by a decision matrix. Although basically subjective, a written decision matrix forces the decision makers to evaluate the alternatives by the same criteria. Although some installations have successfully added a "weighting factor" to each of the selected criteria and used a "final score" to pick the best alternative, other managers have found that such a scheme does not consider individual circumstances or business judgment. One minicomputer system may score higher on a decision matrix but from a strictly business viewpoint may not be worth the price difference from the next-highest minicomputer hardware. An average three-hour response time for maintenance could eliminate a hardware choice that was perfect in all other respects. Whatever scheme or evaluation method is chosen for the subject in question, the goal is to compare each choice logically and professionally. With such an approach, a management team has a better chance of developing a high-quality data processing installation.

THE QUALITY CONTROL ANALYST

Correct decisions, well-designed systems, and high-quality programming are the responsibility of the line managers, but every DP installation which has more than five programmers needs a part-time or full-time quality control analyst. Quality control is as much a skill as systems design, programming, or even management.

To fill this important slot, DP managers should select a senior programmer/analyst who has a strong technical background, is familiar with the major production systems, and can interact tactfully with DP professionals at all levels. He or she should report directly to senior DP management, and his or her opinions should be respected.

A quality-control analyst should have at least five major functions: the extent of each will depend primarily on the needs of each particular data processing environment.

First, he or she should develop methods and procedures to check critical reports which come out of the computer room. This will usually require cooperation with the user groups to obtain balancing information and control numbers that could be checked either manually or automatically before the reports are released. The analyst would design control procedures between application systems, since one common and extremely frustrating source of error is the interface between individual application systems. If the analyst possesses a good technical background, he or she could design ways to catch errors as they occur in production. A transaction file that goes into a six-hour month-end batch run may need record count or hash total balancing before the month-end update. Some jobstreams may need checks to verify that operations has executed the job steps in the correct sequence.

Second, the quality-control analyst should continually evaluate the efficiency of production systems, since one major aspect of the quality of performance of a data processing section is the efficiency of its major production batch jobstreams and on-line interactive processing. A good analyst who knows the application system can sometimes spot major inefficiencies just by observing the production jobstream and examining each program in the system. Significant improvements in a frequently run application system could more than pay the salary of the quality-control analyst!

Third, the analyst should help evaluate new systems and proposed changes to existing applications. He or she need not get into specific technical details of the design of new systems, but rather should suggest changes that would assure the accuracy and timeliness of the new procedures. Simply requiring this second opinion on system design proposals should have a significant improvement in the quality of work done by a system analyst or design team. *After all, the medical profession does not hesitate to make full use of consultation and second opinions, and neither should data processing professionals.*

Fourth, the quality-control analyst is the ideal person to work with DP management in establishing basic programming and operational standards. Because this individual is not directly involved in programming, systems, or operations, he or she can be a valuable "third party" when it comes to disputes and disagreements. Many shops would like to implement standards but find themselves tangled in disputes. The quality-control analyst as a "third party," can effectively solve those disagreements before they require management intervention.

Fifth, and most important, the quality-control analyst should work to promote a feeling of professional pride in all areas of data processing, including programming, operations, and data entry. The DP staff should be told that the newly created position of quality-control analyst shows the importance of data processing to the organization. Also, some people work better when they know their work may be judged at any time by someone outside their particular section.

LIFTING THE CURSE OF PROGRAMMING ABENDS

One important goal of any quality-control analyst is to minimize the disastrous consequences of batch production jobs or on-line tasks that abend and require special attention from the operation, programming, and management staffs. Managers at all levels of data processing frequently complain of production problems which significantly interfere with their daily activities, but even managers may not realize the true impact of those problems on programmers, operators, and users.

The most serious consequences are, of course, for the programmer involved. Abends are notorious for occurring after midnight or on Saturday night when the programmer has plans that do not include spending hours digging through a core dump. If abends occur too often, the disruption of a programmer's personal life may cause severe job dissatisfaction. It is no secret that DP shops which frequently require programmers to work nights and weekends to fix production problems have a high rate of costly personnel turnover.

The time required to fix a production problem is always underestimated. Many times Paul the programmer will come in late the next morning after fixing a production problem at night and will wander from office to office telling his friends what he was doing when they called, how mad his wife was, how much trouble he had getting the core dump printed, how the library was filled when he tried to relink his program, and how the operator made him wait an hour to do the library condense. Paul will also need time to shift his mental gears and return to his programming assignments. If both Paul and his manager are lucky, Paul will not forget any important details when he does return to his original task.

Abends also interfere with the operations section. A DP organization with frequent abends will usually find that its operations staff cannot work to its full efficiency. Production abends also cause a loss of user confidence. When Sharon tells the payroll supervisor that her budget reports were late because of a data exception in the PAY COMPUTE program, the payroll supervisor may begin to wonder about the other processing. Users with little DP orientation tend to think of computer systems like they think of their cars. If they have a car that frequently breaks down, they will consider it a "lemon," the mechanics incompetent, or both. A system that frequently "breaks down" may be considered a "lemon," the DP staff regarded as incompetent, or both. With the growing user involvement in data processing (such as data processing advisory committees in many companies), a loss of user confidence can be very damaging.

A production abend is usually fixed under pressure, at which time the programmer may accidentally make an additional error. The job of "fixing the fix" is more common than most professionals care to admit.

Are production abends something data processing must live with? Or are there preventive measures which can be taken before a system is released for production? The best solution is to add a new dimension to traditional testing procedures on every project or major change. Most programming projects have a final system test using actual or specially created test data designed to prove that the system *can* work. When the last report is balanced, the programmers, analysts, and users describe the system as "tested," congratulate themselves on a job well done (even though it may be a few weeks late), and retire to the cafeteria to celebrate over coffee and doughnuts. Perhaps the analysts and users should adjourn to the cafeteria while the programmers begin their "error testing" phase or try to prove that the system does *not* work.

The programmers who worked on the system are the most familiar with the capabilities and features of the given application. Their entire mental effort has been directed toward making the system work—now the "error testing" phase requires them to shift mental gears and ask the questions that will make the new system fail. By finding and

eliminating those conditions that can cause potential abends, the programmers can "preventively tune" a system and make it far more
reliable.

The "error testing" phase should be designed for a specific application in either the batch or interactive mode and should be based on
questions like these:

1. Can each step in the production run handle a case of "no
input?" A program based on processing payroll edit exceptions will
occasionally find a run with complete payroll input. Every conceivable step in a jobstream, including sorts and utilities, which could
have a no input situation must be tested. A user may select an update
function through an on-line menu, realize he or she wanted the
inquiry function, and close the session. Can the update modules
complete their statistical reporting totals with no input?

2. What happens when a blank transaction input record gets into
the processing? It is better to find out during the "error testing"
phase than at 2:00 A.M. during month-end production.

3. Most inputs have some type of control number, such as a
general ledger or item number. Can the programs handle invalid or
incorrect keys without an abend? If a control field has multiple keys,
such as account and store number, what will happen if one part is
correct and the other is invalid?

4. Can the system and programs handle a volume far larger than
that predicted by the analysts and users? Master files and transaction
files seem to grow magically before anyone realizes their impact. A
common error is to have counters that can only hold a predicted
number of records, such as 99,999. The programmer who is on duty
the night record number 100,000 is created will have a definite problem. Counters should be large enough to handle any conceivable
number.

5. Does the program check each division calculation for a potential zero-divide calculation? A programmer who assumes the number
of employees in a cost center will never be zero will be in trouble
when the company sets up a cost center for tax purposes only.

6. Some programs make use of internal tables to hold variable
numbers of data elements. For example, if the personnel manager has
a long-standing habit of requesting only three summary reports, and
the programmer feels safe to make a table of 10 report requests,

what will happen when the new personnel manager submits 11 report requests? All internal tables should be protected by program tests to guarantee they will not be loaded or accessed outside of their limits.

7. Most systems require that their master or detail input files be processed in a predetermined sequence. If a sort step fails and an unsorted file goes into a batch program, will that module catch the error and give enough information so that operations can correct the problem themselves? Programs which require sorted input can give unfathomable logic or data errors when the input is not sorted correctly.

8. Have all data been checked for validity? Does the program assume that data coming from another system will be in the correct format, with packed decimal fields always signed, and numbers in the correct range? What will happen if that assumption is not correct?

9. Have all end-of-file conditions been tested? If the system test had the transaction file read end-of-file first, will the program handle the master file reaching end-of-file before the transaction file? Does the end-of-file logic require certain record types to come in a special sequence, and will the logic fail or loop if one of those record types is missing?

10. Some programs use the date from the machine or from control cards provided by an operator, control clerk, or user. If the control clerk submits a card with the year "0," will the program abend or inform the operator of the error? The same problem can happen with any type of input from CRTs.

These are only a few of the more common errors which can result in program abends and system failures. A group of experienced programmers should be able to develop additional questions appropriate to their own systems.

There is a price to pay in terms of human and computer resources by adding an "error testing" phase to the final testing cycle of any project. However, management should weigh the cost of this extra testing effort against the problems that result from the curse of program abends.

THE QUALITY OF COMMUNICATION

Many of the so-called problems of quality control in both business and scientific data processing can be traced directly to poor human communication, and likewise many of the outstandingly successful projects can be charged to good communication. Data processing experts all too often ignore their communication skills with other professionals, their own managers, and users in the organization. To be blunt, some DP people have very poor skills in written and oral communication.

This unfortunate situation should not be surprising considering the background of most senior professionals and data processing managers. Technical people are not generally known for their communication skills. The popular myth of computer experts is that they sit alone in tiny, cluttered offices interacting in a frenzied manner with computer terminals, and stopping only for meals and trips to the restroom. Universities help generate these myths by not presenting students with a realistic picture of what to expect in the business world. Businesses themselves seldom publish accurate position descriptions which inform prospective programmer/analysts that they will probably spend only 20 percent of their time over a one-year period using those technical skills learned at the university. The rest of the time will be spent working with users, interacting with the operations section, reporting to management, completing paperwork, investigating problems, answering questions, and so on. Of course, there are exceptions, and some programmers and programmer/analysts do spend a majority of their time performing the specific technical work they have been trained for.

Although most DP positions depend on oral and written communication, most organizations do not provide any communication training, and the professional staff will stumble along using trial-and-error techniques in their communication activities. Since DP managers usually come from the ranks of those professionals who use trial and error, their own management level skills may be sadly lacking in productive and efficient human communication abilities. When communication itself suffers, so does the quality of the systems managed by those executives. Just as new DP managers are seldom taught the techniques and principles of management as a profession, DP professionals at all levels are seldom taught to develop their communication skills, and the quality of their own work suffers.

Senior company executives are often the first to complain about poor communication from the senior DP management team. The

data processing people may realize that, if they add a new on-line accounts payable system, the response time of the current order entry
system will be terrible until management approves another meg of
core. The senior vice-president, however, may not understand the
relationship between the on-line loading factor and response time
until the order entry manager howls in protest at his nine- or ten-
second response time. Why didn't the DP manager make this problem
known? A project leader may understand that the estimate to upgrade the sales reporting system will depend primarily upon test-time
availability, but the DP manager who makes a commitment to the
sales division has forgotten the hassles of getting adequate test time
during the on-line day or at the end of the month. Why didn't the
project leader mention this important factor? No one is right and no
one is wrong—the problem is that people on both sides failed to communicate clearly and completely.

Communication skills can be developed over a period of time by
a conscious, direct effort. Every faulty communication which affects
the quality of a project, report, or decision should be recognized by
the people involved, and the "egoless managers" should take the lead
by calmly pointing out their own mistakes. If the manager involved
can admit a lack of skill in the area of communication, the employees
will quickly learn that poor written and verbal communication is a
common problem in the world of data processing and can be rectified
by hard work and individual initiative.

8

Reducing System Maintenance

More than half the programming budget in many data processing installations is devoted to "maintenance programming"—that nebulous, hard-to-define activity known as "keeping the system running." One frequently quoted estimate is that by the mid-1980s this system maintenance function will require 60 to 80 percent of the available programming talent. Even now, it is not unusual for the maintenance of some business application systems to cost a company more in one year than it cost the department to develop the application systems in the first place. The factors that caused the situation are interesting from a historical viewpoint but are largely irrelevant to a management team which wonders why it takes more programmers to support a system than it took to create the original application, and why a seemingly trivial change can take weeks to accomplish. Such concerns are truly relevant in the 1980s, and data processing management must be prepared to meet those concerns. Even the advent of sophisticated data base management systems has not lowered the maintenance burden in some installations, contrary to original goals.

The DP manager may feel helpless in controlling system maintenance costs. After all, isn't the maintenance burden intrinsic to data processing? Even if an application system required continual, expensive maintenance, isn't it better just to accept reality and pay the price until the system can be rewritten?

The answer is an unqualified "no." Systems and programming maintenance costs can be reduced by a manager who is willing to take a long, hard look at his or her entire organization, and perhaps challenge some traditional DP procedures. A project to reduce system maintenance costs will involve careful planning, thorough research, and forceful implementation. In fact, some reorganization of the DP department may be necessary to fully accomplish such a goal.

High maintenance costs are not intrinsic to the business data processing world; rather, they were caused by system and management errors when data processing was young and unproven. They are tolerated now in part because they have become familiar to most installations, and in part because changing this situation requires strong management commitment.

An additional benefit of reducing system maintenance costs (aside from improving the bottom-line P&L) is that DP managers will probably improve the morale and productivity of their entire programming section. Most programmers and analysts would prefer to work on development projects rather than maintenance, and most DP managers would rather use their programming resources to help satisfy the ever-increasing demands from user groups. Since "maintenance" in data processing seems to have the same connotation as the Black Death had in the Middle Ages, a better term for that function would be *production support.* Maintenance is the frustrating, exasperating, complicated, and frequently dull task of keeping someone else's programs running; production support can be defined as maintenace that has been managed, controlled, and perfected from a true business viewpoint. It may not be fun, but it will not be fatal. Moreover, shops with costly maintenance tend to have high rates of personnel turnover, as the professional staff becomes bored and moves to positions which promise new development work.

It is essential that the DP manager prepare the professional staff before beginning a project to reduce system and programming maintenance. Obviously, the systems and programming staff will be intimately involved in such a project, and its extra efforts will be a determining factor in the success or failure of the project.

Supporting existing systems is a vital and necessary part of data processing, and most professionals can take pride in it if the maintenance function is approached as a task to be managed, which means the more frustrating portions are reduced and the more interesting aspects are increased. Production support can and should be looked upon as a science. Maintaining other people's systems may never be attractive, but the way in which that support is performed can become very challenging and even interesting. Management should stress that any additional demands placed on programmers—such as extra paperwork—will be justified in the end by a reduction in the maintenance burden.

A program to reduce system maintenance costs usually has three separate but overlapping stages:

1   Measuring the existing maintenance effort.
2   Summarizing and analyzing the maintenance activity.
3   Resolving the maintenance problems by order of priority.

Such a project is similar to the systems analysis procedure in which the DP profession attempts to help various user groups. In this case, however, DP professionals will be attempting to help themselves and their company by applying the scientific method to help increase their own productivity. This experience should be very educational for all DP professionals who are engaged in systems analysis and design work. Again, such an approach is possible only when the executive team tries to follow the "egoless management" philosophy and is willing to critically examine themselves and their long-standing procedures.

MEASURE THE MAINTENANCE EFFORT

The first step in any measurement process is to define the activity to be measured. System maintenance, however, is one of those required activities everyone dislikes but no one can define.

For example, a given task may be classified as "development" when interviewing a prospective analyst but defined as maintenance when asking the controller for a larger DP budget. The guiding question should be: Is this task necessary to keep the application system running in a sound, professional manner?

If the answer is yes, that task or activity is indeed part of the maintenance effort and is not correctly defined as development or enhancement. Such typical programmer and analyst actions as answering questions from users, rearranging data on a report, adding badly needed transactions to an update program, and making logic fixes are examples of system maintenance.

Maintenance or production support requests should be divided into *required* and *optional.* Required tasks are those necessary to satisfy reasonable production support needs, and optional requests can be delayed or never implemented without seriously affecting the users. When performing detailed analysis of the maintenance function, as described later in this chapter, it will be important to separate these two activities. The former can only be controlled, but the latter can be successfully managed.

Because of the high degree of judgment involved in separating maintenance from development, the DP manager himself may elect to categorize each activity, or he or she may appoint one senior-level professional to be the final judge. It is very important that the standards are consistently and fairly applied in each case. There may never be industry-wide agreement on the definitions of maintenance and development, or of required maintenance, as opposed to optional production support. As long as each installation follows consistent guidelines, communication among professionals will be reasonably accurate.

A time- and project-accounting system is the ideal method with which to collect the basic data on system maintenance. However, average time-accounting systems (either in-house or purchased as a software package) may have serious deficiencies, either in the way they are structured or in the way they are implemented. They are often of marginal value because they don't have enough categories and because the existing categories are so vague that they are all-inclusive. If the categories are not properly defined and do not match a shop's typical activities, the programmers may spend more time trying to accurately categorize an activity than the task took in the first place. If definitions are vague, difficult, or virtually impossible, perhaps examples would be more useful and practical. People can more easily relate to specific examples than to complex, ambiguous descriptions. Since programmers are more interested in job satisfaction and reward from DP-oriented projects than in paperwork, they will soon learn to gloss over paperwork requirements in favor of more productive work.

Some of the typical but sometimes overlooked maintenance actions include:

1 Answering phone calls and having personal meetings with users.
2 Helping the operating staff with production questions.
3 Doing the paperwork necessary to keep the system running.
4 Tracking down errors in reports.
5 Correcting errors and rewriting application system documentation.
6 Performing reruns and restarts of production jobs, including after-hours work.
7 Following up on production problems.
8 Running special jobs that are under programmer control.
9 Investigating complex logic errors or researching the details of system processing.

If the time-accounting system does not include these activities as maintenance, it must be examined and upgraded before it can be used in any serious study of DP maintenance activity or production support.

Even with a well-designed, comprehensive time- and project-accounting system, the DP manager may find problems. In the average DP environment, the time-accounting system is the last production job done during a cycle, and the reports usually sit on a desk until someone bothers to file them. Members of the professional staff soon discover the lack of importance of time accounting and become careless in monitoring their own time. Time-accounting jobs should be treated as production, and the professional staff should be made aware of the new purpose behind the time-accounting system: that data is not being collected to be ignored, but to be used as part of a serious, ongoing study.

PERSONAL LOGS

As a by-product of any valid time-accounting system, the participants will be forced to maintain a log of their weekly activities. These "personal logs" will be just as important as the actual time-accounting summary reports, since any qualitative analysis of the maintenance effort must focus on the specific activities of that effort. Discovering that a programmer spent 70 percent of her time on maintenance is one thing, but knowing what that 70 percent consisted of is even more valuable.

Although the format of the log should be standardized (with name, time, and activity), the actual contents should be left up to the individual, as long as it is readable and accurate. This log approach should be implemented along with the time-accounting system.

Again, it is vital that management give the staff some feedback from the logs and the accounting reports, even if it is a simple, "I can't read this line." Without feedback, the professional staff will never realize the importance of the study and the entire data-collection process.

At this point, DP management may encounter overt resistance from the professional staff, especially as it relates to the extra paperwork and the perception that the study has been triggered by a suspicion "that some people aren't doing their jobs." The extra paperwork is indeed a burden on a busy staff, but management should emphasize the value of the study.

The uneasy feeling caused by any study of professional activity can be alleviated by stressing that maintenance is a widespread problem in most DP shops, and that a study of maintenance effort is literally a state-of-the-art project. An interesting sidelight to the use of personal logs is that management may then be able to estimate the hardware resources being used in the maintenance effort. Despite what many programmers think, computer time is not free, and some DP managers will be surprised to learn how many resources they have tied up in "maintenance."

ANALYZE THE MAINTENANCE

Once the data-collection and personal-log procedures are in place, DP management may be tempted to start attacking the apparent causes of the high maintenance effort. This impulse is usually premature, since the true causes of a high maintenance effort may not show up immediately. Rather, long-term study and analysis may be necessary to discover important patterns and trends.

For example, an input error caused by lack of editing in an accounts payable program may cause a high maintenance effort one week but may in fact not occur again for another few years. By devoting his or her limited resources on that one problem, the DP manager may miss the more expensive and common maintenance problems. *True management thinking should be concerned with long-range and reoccurring problems rather than limited immediate problems.*

During the data collection process, DP management should have contact with the rank-and-file programming and system staff to explain and encourage the system collection project. But the communication should travel both ways—production-minded programmers can provide a wealth of information which will be useful during the analysis phase of the project. The "egoless management" attitude will allow such two-way communication without threatening the management staff.

For example, if programmer John Jones asks if his unofficial job of helping balance the payroll register every few weeks is a "maintenance task," the DP manager should carefully make note of it. The manager may have never known that the payroll supervisor required such help! Such comments and information will help the manager get a feel for questions that will arise during the analysis phase.

Any study of maintenance effort should also cover those staff members not normally thought of as part of the maintenance team, such as first-line managers and systems analysts. If any part of their time is spent in supporting production, their log sheets should be included in the time-accounting and data collection process.

The analysis of the project can begin after two months' collection of raw data. This step is designed to summarize both the quantitative aspects of maintenance (the time-accounting reports) and the qualitative portion (the personal logs). A summary of time-accounting reports may show that the maintenance effort is cyclical. That is, month-end or quarter-end periods require more maintenance hours. This information is valuable in planning development projects where certain staff members have dual development and maintenance responsibilities. In those shops with permanent teams of maintenance programmers, the cyclical trends may show that during certain periods some labor is actually wasted.

Management should use the quantitative data to determine the correlation, if any, between high maintenance activity and turnover.

If the shop does indeed have such a correlation, management can predict which individuals are likely to leave and thus take preventive measures, such as salary adjustments and rotation of assignments.

The qualitative information contained in the personal logs should be summarized by an experienced project leader or senior programmer who is familiar with both the application systems and shop procedures. This summary needs to have a minimum amount of interpretation and a maximum amount of pattern analysis. In other words, the summary should indicate trends in maintenance patterns which remain consistent over the long term. This pattern analysis might be arranged by application system, such as an accounts receivable system that needs continual updates to the aging calculations or an inventory system that requires continual programmer intervention to handle specific requests from user groups. Or perhaps the summary will be arranged by operational problems, such as incomplete restart instructions that require programmers to become involved in restarts and reruns.

The trend analysis should be performed independently by several individuals, each taking a one- or two-week period to summarize the results. Naturally, some analysis of the causes of maintenance effort will be integrated into the summaries—this is unavoidable. However, the final analysis will be conducted by management with results of the separate summaries provided by the senior staff. Allowing different individuals to contribute to the maintenance evaluation will assure that no major aspects of maintenance will be missed during the final analysis.

Both the senior staff and management should note that maintenance can always be divided into "unavoidable maintenance" and "avoidable maintenance." Updating state tax tables in a payroll system is required by law, but the process by which that updating takes place can be analyzed for efficiency—there is a significant difference between a procedure that takes 10 minutes and a procedure that requires several hours.

ATTACK THE CAUSES

After several months of data collection and analysis, management should feel confident enough to begin attacking the causes of costly system maintenance. The priority list should be determined not only by which problem leads to the most expensive system maintenance effort, but also by factors such as degree of problem (an incorrect payroll run may be a political disaster for data processing), associated morale problems (a programmer called in to fix the same error week after week may be the next programmer to quit), and availability of resources.

This last factor may be the single most important limitation in developing any priority list. For example, if the general ledger system is the single most expensive system from a maintenance view but the general ledger experts are busy on another project, the maintenance problem will simply have to wait.

There are a number of common system maintenance problems that can affect almost any business DP installation to a degree, but the specific causes of high maintenance are still usually unique to a particular shop.

One area of unnecessary programmer maintenance is in operational support, usually with reruns, restarts, and requests from operations for help. Obviously, any application system can and will abend because of bad tapes, disk failures, software errors, and operator mistakes, but each jobstream should be documented enough so that members of the operations staff can handle the common problems themselves. Not only does programmer involvement in the computer room take valuable programmer hours, but it can also be a major source of friction between the programming and operations sections.

Adding restart and rerun documentation to production jobstreams involves substantial resources, but costs may be regained in less than a year. Also, such a task can offer an excellent training opportunity for new programmers, or for experienced programmer/analysts who are learning these systems and shop procedures.

Too often, however, operational documentation is useless because it is not usefully organized. For example, operations "run sheets" typically contain detailed data set or file information, but not specific, cookbook-style restart instructions which can be quickly followed by an operator or shift supervisor.

Before any major documentation is undertaken as part of a plan to reduce system maintenance, management should carefully reevaluate the current type and style of documentation. Good, simple operational documentaion can significantly reduce programming involvement in day-to-day operational problems.

USER SUPPORT

A second area of usually unnecessary programmer and analyst maintenance effort is in the area of user support. Answering questions regarding reports, data entry, transactions, and system usage are all parts of a maintenance burden which should be examined.

It may be impossible or politically inadvisable to discourage users from asking questions about application systems, but the DP manager can reduce this burden by verifying that each production system has clear, easy-to-use documentation, which explains the system from the user viewpoint. It may be necessary to ask another part of the company, such as the sales or advertising division, for assistance in reviewing written documentation for clarity.

Another solution might be to select one professional or paraprofessional to serve as a single production liaison. This would then free other staff from continual interruptions. It may not be evident from a time-accounting report, but a day interrupted by seven phone calls from various users is a day that has been severely disrupted if the programmer was deeply involved in a task requiring concentrated mental effort.

A third area of programmer activity which affects almost all DP installations is the difficulty in making changes to existing application systems. Whereas adding a new report or transaction code to a system may be thought of as development, in many cases such a development task turns out to be a maintenance nightmare. Not only is it a difficult, time-consuming project, but also, errors usually result from these new features and require extensive maintenance effort just to keep production running.

Such "simple" changes can cause severe problems because DP management does not control the efficiency of system maintenance changes. In fact, *most DP shops perform maintenance changes in an archaic, inefficient manner which would not be tolerated by any other division of the company.*

The entire change process can be simplified and made more reliable by realizing that changes to any application system are rarely unique.

For example, during the seven-year life of a non-data base payroll system, there may be 15 requests to add new data fields to the payroll master file. Yet in each maintenance (or "development") project, the analyst or programmer usually must reinvent the wheel by first determining how to accomplish the required change.

The answer is usually a list of 10 or 20 or 30 specific steps written on a scrap coding form. After the maintenance task is completed, the programmer usually discards the list, and the next programmer must go through the entire mental effort again.

Programmers and analysts usually do not retain documentation showing how a particular change was made; rather, they congratulate themselves if they have updated the user documentation correctly. Management should insist that any written documentation developed during a maintenance project be copied for a permanent system file. This requirement alone should save a substantial amount of time in future maintenance changes.

Furthermore, with specific steps documented, the programmer and analyst will be better able to ensure the correctness of the change, and this should result in fewer maintenance problems.

PRODUCTION CHANGES

A fourth area requiring high maintenance which is often overlooked involves continuous changes to production systems. The DP manager should examine the time-accounting and personal log summaries for instances in which programmers had to recompile and relink production programs. Since production systems should be generally static, the manager must ask why the programming staff needs to make continual changes to keep the system running.

Are the changes designed to bypass batches of data that were inputted by mistake? A control card and some simple bypass logic would accomplish the same result with much less programmer effort and time. Do the programs need to be modified to trigger certain reports and options that are not user controlled? Perhaps the system needs a new transaction code or method for the user to select and trigger reports himself.

Even data base management systems require analysis of the maintenance requirements. Since the age of true "data independence" is still some years away (perhaps in the recently introduced relational data base systems), systems analysts evaluating DBMS packages must require the vendors to explain just what it takes to add a new data element to a data base. Another important question is the difficulty of adding additional relationships as a means of "navigating" through the data base. If the merchandising staff wants to use pricepoint as a "key" to accessing item records, how much effort will that take in both people and machine time?

THE QUESTION OF CONTROL

DP managers may wonder if they can go too far in giving up control over certain application systems. Some analysts and DP professionals adhere to the seldom-stated but often-followed theory that certain application systems need DP staff control and cannot be entrusted to users. They might argue that certain options and updating should be controlled by a programmer familiar with the system and its internal processing.

Such an argument ignores the real world of data processing. While a system is being developed, it is true that the programmers and analysts know the system better than any user group and would prefer to trigger critical system action themselves. After all, the system is still relatively new, and the technical people are anxious to help bring the system into full production status.

But the programmer who wrote that critical update process will eventually leave and be replaced by a programmer who lacks not only the detailed knowledge of that particular system but also the desire to trigger a weekly update or critical report run. The new programmer treats that requirement as a maintenance burden. The original reason for preserving data processing control over that production application system no longer exists, and the DP staff is stuck with one more maintenance burden for the next 10 years.

A general policy should be to transfer as much system control to the user groups as is practical and safe. Ideally, the user management should control the system without DP professional staff assistance or involvement. Contrary to the beliefs of some data processors, users can be trusted with application systems if they are given the proper documentation and training.

By examining systems which do require continual programmer intervention, the DP manager can develop a plan to transfer control over the system operation from the programmers to the user groups, where it belongs, and correct a mistake made long ago when the system was first developed.

WHEN DOES MAINTENANCE STOP?

Data processing professionals at all levels—from programmers to MIS directors—have been conditioned to accept the philosophy of application system maintenance with the same fervor that the accounting profession has accepted the principle of double-entry bookkeeping. Yet, from a management-level viewpoint, it is difficult for DP managers to justify some of the "optional" requests for changes, fixes, and enhancements. One way to significantly reduce maintenance costs is to examine critically the philosophy and history behind the entire system maintenance problem.

The purpose of any application system is to satisfy a specific business need, which usually involves satisfying the user or user group who controls that need. The accounting department determines the acceptability of the financial reports, and its staff must use those reports in its daily operations. Since nothing in the world of data processing is ever perfect, the accounting people will find inconsistencies, incompatibilities, and slight omissions which they feel should be corrected. The balance report may need a fix to accommodate customers with cash flow problems. The accounting reports may never be 100 percent perfect as defined by the accounting department. The sales department may never be completely satisfied with the sales analysis reports. The new planning manager may want major changes in the profit planning models. The order entry personnel may want another relationship in the order entry data base so they can scan for orders by costing code. Users are usually not completely satisfied. Such dissatisfaction may come from a desire to do their jobs better, or a desire to save themselves unnecessary work, or just a perfectly human desire to make things better. Whatever the reason, many users want changes one week and changes to the changes the next week.

Data processing as a profession has responded by automatically directing its resources toward making the corrections requested by the users. Many maintenance changes were approved because of the natural tendency to make people happy. If Jerry the accounting manager wanted the cutoff date moved to the bottom of the page, a programmer would do it. If Helen in the sales department wanted to increase the number of lines printed on the daily sales report to save paper, it would be done. In the terms of behavior theory, the user was rewarded for asking for a change by having it completed, and the programmer was rewarded for his or her effort by a verbal pat-on-the-back from the user. The DP manager smiled at Helen and told her they were more than happy to help. Two weeks later Helen was back with another request: Could the final sales total be printed on the first page of the report? The "maintenance cycle" had begun to feed on itself.

Obviously, some requests are more justified than others. The key to breaking the maintenance cycle is to use sound business judgment as the basis for assigning priorities. DP management should estimate the cost of a maintenance change based on rates of $30 or $35 per hour and then decide if the change is worth the price. Certainly Helen would like the final sales figure printed on the first page to save her from looking through the entire report. Jerry prefers to have the cutoff data at the bottom of the page where the important numbers are located. Both of these requests are valid from the user's viewpoint and would help them do their own jobs better. The management dilemma is that neither request may be justified in terms of a basic cost-benefits decision. The account change may cost two hours, or $70, and the sales reporting change may cost ten hours, or $350, not counting the cost in computer time. Are these changes worth the price not only in terms of direct programmer time, but in terms of other high priority projects that these programmers could have been working on?

Lost opportunities are sometimes even more costly than the actual time spent on maintenance fixes. DP management should put this complicated question honestly and fairly before the user involved: Does the accounting manager want to allocate one programmer to make minor modifications to an existing system or to work full time on the on-line cash application system which has been on the drawing board for two years. The choice for both managers is between many small and relatively minor improvements and waiting for a major but longer payback project. With the growing involvement of the more sophisticated users in data processing policy, DP managers at all levels must start an immediate education program to teach user managers the true cost of data processing activities and the "maintenance dilemma." The exact nature and format of this educational project will vary with each company and even with each user, but the primary goal must be to share with the users the complex and frustrating problem of allocating scarce and expensive professional resoures.

Although senior management can assume the responsibility for determining the business justification for each requested fix, enhancement, or addition, such a policy is the fastest way to lose friends and influence people the wrong way. The more productive policy is to educate the individual users as to the true cost of researching insignificant problems and making relatively minor system changes. Well-educated and sophisticated users are excellent allies in the struggle to help crack the maintenance nightmare.

9

The DP Technical Audit: A Do-It-Yourself Project

A few weeks spent in a do-it-yourself technical audit can garner valuable savings in terms of people and machine productivity. With the ever-increasing inflationary squeeze on DP budgets, an internal technical DP audit can eliminate unnecessary production, discover redundant effort, and even recover valuable machine resources. In almost every centralized or distributed data processing installation, knowledgeable technical people can always find inefficiencies and wasteful practices that have gone unnoticed for years. In the 1970s, DP and corporate management could easily tolerate such waste, but in the 1980s, company management will demand that all DP hardware and software resources are used to their maximum potential.

The purpose of such an internal audit is not to question current management policies and practices, but rather to examine the detailed technical operation of a data center and recommend how those technical resources can be better used. One advantage of the "egoless management" philosophy is that the management staff is mature enough to allow employees to make important suggestions without feeling threatened or insecure. Such a management team is more concerned with improving total departmental performance than worrying about how it looks to have employees telling their managers how to run their shops.

Such an internal audit is also an excellent training project for the professional staff to gain new insight and knowledge about departmental procedures. The staff chosen as part of the audit team should also develop a new sense of "business awareness" which will help develop more responsible programmers and analysts.

DP management considering such an internal technical audit should evaluate several factors before making a decision to start. Internal technical DP audits are a new concept in data processing, and they have drawbacks as well as benefits.

First, internal audits by a DP staff require at least three experienced programmers, programmer/analysts, or system analysts for at least five days of full-time effort. This may require other projects or assignments to be postponed. Counting the planning and follow-up effort by the management and the audit staff, the project will easily require at least 20 days of time. The time lost may be even greater than the actual count, because the people involved in an internal audit tend to be the more experienced and productive.

Second, the attitude of the audit team is the major factor in determining the success of the project. DP management should select senior staff members who have some tact and can interact responsibly with all levels of data processing and user group organizations. Each member of the team must be told individually that although he or she will have significant responsibility and power the success of the project rests primarily on the cooperation they can elicit from the staff. Without full cooperation and support from the programming, systems, operational, and user sections, the audit team will encounter resistance, and the project will, at best, have limited success. Most likely, it will be a waste of time.

Third, an internal DP audit is not meant to take the place of a professional, independent audit by accountants or management consultants. However, experience shows that most standard audits of data processing simply do not delve into enough technical detail. Unfortunately, many final audit reports contain the three classic recommendations: (1) "keep the programmers out of the computer room"; (2) "produce more documentation"; and (3) "support motherhood and apple pie." The era of the true DP auditors who can test production systems, evaluate DP management control, and provide technical recommendations is still several years in the future.

Fourth, internal DP audits should be justified to management on the basis of actual machine and people resource savings, and senior management must carefully track the recommendations from the audit to their eventual implementation. This measurement process will be excellent training for the staff involved in the audit, since very few technical professionals outside of the senior management ranks have an opportunity to apply business concepts to the data processing function.

Fifth, a successful do-it-yourself technical audit should be proposed as a yearly "tune-up" for the entire DP organization, much as the family car needs a yearly tune-up to retain its operating efficiency. In the same way, a do-it-yourself technical audit can pinpoint current problem areas, eliminate unnecessary processing, and tighten up daily operational procedures.

CHOOSING THE AUDIT TEAM

The first tendency of management is to choose members of the first- or second-level management group for the internal audit team. After all, an experienced project leader or programming supervisor should know the application systems, shop procedures, and current management policies. He or she is, however, a member of management, and for that reason alone should not be on the audit staff. The months or years of participation in policymaking and departmental procedures will tend to make that person at least partially biased toward existing procedures. The audit team needs professionals who tend not to be naturally biased toward current systems and procedures that they themselves have developed or for which they have taken responsibility.

The best candidates are senior programmer/analysts who have at least one year's experience in the organization and who have shown an interest in management-level activities. Both a system design and maintenance background are equally valuable for a good internal auditor. A senior programmer who tends to be inquisitive and resourceful is preferable to one who has conformed to all management directives. In other words, a good audit staff must be composed of professionals who are not afraid to disagree with management.

At the same time, members of the audit team must be tactful. A senior programmer who has difficulty dealing with people is not suitable for this position and would cause friction and resentment which could destroy the positive results of the entire project.

Being appointed to an audit project, even for a few days, should be regarded as a privilege for the best performers in the shop. The experience itself is excellent training for those who may someday be promoted to a first-level supervisory position. Three staff members are enough for small and medium-sized shops, but a large data processing organization may require up to seven professionals to complete the job in the week allotted.

The audit team should report directly to the DP director or manager for the duration of the project, which includes both the audit project and the following evaluation and recommendation period.

DELIVERABLES

Every project or activity in data processing needs well-defined goals that can be used as the measure of success. The first phase of a payroll project, for example, may have a written set of functional specifications as the project deliverables. A project to add a new transaction to the inventory system might have 10 deliverables, including sample test results and user documentation. A do-it-yourself technical audit should deliver a written report with suggestions and recommendations for improving the technical operation of the systems and operating procedures. The format of the report does not need to be defined until completion of the audit phase of the project and can be left up to the audit staff.

PLANNING THE AUDIT PROJECT

Management must give the audit staff enough time to develop a written plan for the entire day-by-day audit procedure. Usually two-hour blocks of time are a fine enough planning unit. The purpose of this detailed schedule is to prevent the audit project from becoming a long, never-ending project. During the planning process, senior management should work with the staff and provide consultation and review when necessary, but the schedule and choice of systems to be examined should be left to the audit staff themselves.

The plan should begin with a list of the application systems and proceed to the general shop procedures and policies that affect production systems and testing procedures. The goal of the audit team should be to find areas which can be made less costly and more trouble free. If the audit staff understands that computer time is money, and that the quality of their recommendations will be judged from a business standpoint, then the plan and the final report will be worthwhile documents.

A technical internal DP audit will usually involve at least three major areas: (1) efficiency in production systems, (2) input and output processing, and (3) documentation. The audit staff can and should examine additional aspects of the department based on their experience and knowledge of the organization and its specific problems. For example, a shop with on-line processing will have different characteristics than one which primarily has batch processing.

EFFICIENCY IN PRODUCTION SYSTEMS

Virtually all production systems have some degree of inefficiency, because "efficiency in production" is usually a minor design goal. Older, well-established systems may have major inefficiencies because the original programming or analyst staff did not fully understand the application or because the operational environment has changed significantly. For example, shops which converted from IBM DOS to an OS operating system may have done so without regard to the potential extra features of the OS environment. For example, new disk drives may offer capabilities which are not used.

Just a few of the common problems in the typical batch-oriented business production systems which can be examined by an internal technical audit team are:

1   The greatest single potential time waster of all—sorts.
Sorting takes 25 percent or more of the total run time in many business shops, but most professionals give little consideration to sort ef-

ficiency. Although many shops purchase special sort packages superior to the standard vendor-provided sorts, management may not realize that operational changes can also improve sort productivity. Some simple ways to improve sorting efficiency are:

(a)   Verify that all sort work areas on disk are fully distributed on all available devices. Sorts run much faster when serious device contention is reduced, and it is amazing how many daily and weekly sorts are not set up for maximum device efficiency.

(b)   Eliminate unnecessary sort fields. The original system design may have included control or reporting fields which are still used for sorting but make little difference in the current system environment. Reducing sort fields can save on both CPU and I/O resources.

(c)   Consider the use of a merge rather than a sort when two files must be sorted and then merged into one large file. If one data set is already sorted, it is wasteful to sort that same file again just to merge it with a second one. A better procedure is to sort the other file and then merge the two sorted data sets together. In this case, two steps are more efficient than one.

(d)   Consider the use of disk rather than tape to hold input and output files. Older batch systems may have been designed by analysts who were still functioning in the older "tape" mode of data processing. Small files can and should be put on disk rather than tape, which will not only save considerable I/O time but also will reduce the chance for manual intervention errors and hardware problems. When questioned about situations where small files are on tape rather than disk, most operational and systems managers scratch their heads and explain that no one ever bothered to question that situation!

(e)   Consider running large sort steps as separate jobs, rather than as a job step in a larger production job. Some system designs produce large files which need to be sorted but are not processed again until farther down in the job sequence. It may save valuable time in those critical production jobstreams to have a separate sort job that can run simultaneously with the original job and have the large file sorted by the time the original job needs that sorted data set. Although adding more jobs will tend to complicate production, by having "simultaneous" sorts the run time on a critical production system can be improved significantly. This is especially true for those situations where large disk resources are hard to find and the sort can be run at a point in the job schedule when such disk resources are more available. Even if the application system is not so time critical, the audit team should determine whether "simultaneous" sorts will significantly improve scheduling by allowing other time-critical jobs to be started earlier.

(f) Study the sort manual for simple ways to increase sort efficiency. The time required may not be justified to improve just one sort, but if that improvement can be made in all of the shop's sorts, the total efficiency gained may justify the time spent studying the sort manual. A 2 percent decrease in run time for one sort is not significant, but a daily 2 percent time saving is impressive, and will free additional resources.

2 Evaluate the steps for creating backup files.

The need for a backup, or copy, of a tape master file is too frequently realized only after the system is in production. The support programmer (or operational support technician) will then add a step which simply copies the data set onto another tape or disk. This procedure is simple and requires no JCL changes, but it is also inefficient. A better method is to modify the original program to write out two copies of the file in question. The time savings will be significant, especially when several jobs in a DP section are thus modified.

3 Analyze the device contention in both disk and tape jobs.

Maintenance to existing systems usually means adding new files and processing to existing programs, and more often than not, the files are added with little thought to the total system integration. This is usually true when the maintenance programmer does not consider or even understand the total system flow before designing the additional processing. All jobs with permanent disk files should be analyzed for device contention that will slow down the total job and shop processing. Disk files in general should be spread across all available packs to reduce both channel and device contention. This examination should be done at least once a year.

4 Question all reports that may not be necessary.

Producing reports is a major part of any business system, and the audit team should verify that all daily, weekly, and monthly reports for a particular application system are necessary. Too often, as user requirements change or managers are replaced in user departments, the reporting requirements for a system are not reevaluated, and some reports delivered to the user sections are never even read. In other cases, users may not even know that a valuable report exists. For those DP shops that have never taken a close, hard look at their reports, the paper savings alone for a year may pay the cost of the entire internal DP audit!

Installations which use report generator or query languages to produce reports from on-line data base files should examine alternatives—a high-level language such as COBOL may create a standard daily report more efficiently than a query language.

5   Evaluate disk space requirements for all application systems.

When systems are put in production for the first time, the programmer or system analyst must often guess the eventual size of the transactions and report files on disk. Since systems generally grow in size, one might expect a common problem to be a lack of disk space. Whereas that situation does exist, the solution—increasing the disk space—may lead to an even more serious problem if large amounts of disk space are allocated to files which are never used. In many cases, a programmer or operations technician who fixes a space problem will allocate far greater space than is necessary. This can cause production problems when jobs are fighting each other to acquire space they do not really need, and the entire production schedule may suffer.

6   Examine the operational documentation for each system.

Operational instructions are vital for reruns or restarts of production jobs, and a DP organization which has poor operational documentation usually pays the price in terms of incorrect restarts and reruns, unnecessary operator intervention, and expensive programmer involvement. The audit team should evaluate all production system documentation for correctness and usefulness. This examination will be welcomed by the operational staff, as their needs for documentation and instructions are often overlooked.

7   Study the control and balancing procedures that are in place for each major application system.

If a production system has balancing procedures performed by control clerks or the operational staff, the audit team should evaluate the usefulness and purpose of each procedure. Occasionally, a manual procedure will duplicate an automatic system check or simply be worthless. In other cases, major production problems may result from a lack of control procedures, especially in the critical interfaces between application systems.

Balance and control procedures are far more complex than most system analysts understand, and it is hard to determine which aspects of a system should be controlled. Some professionals go overboard and suggest manual or automatic balance procedures for all parts of a system. Others may not believe that manual or automatic controls are useful. Although the audit staff cannot do more than make spot recommendations for controls in certain systems, such a focus of attention may lead to future cost-efficient control procedures.

8   Analyze the file access methods of the major, long-running systems as well as the smaller, daily systems.

Application systems are often designed around certain assumptions, such as the number of input transactions, or the size of the master file records. When the system grows over the years, and processing requirements change the environment, these original assumptions may become obsolete. The file access methods which are derived from those assumptions will be inefficient.

For example, a general ledger input edit may use direct access to validate the account number, which is reasonable if the batch has only several thousand records. However, if the batches have grown to an average of 50,000 or 100,000 records in random account number sequence, the time required to directly access the chart of accounts file may be significant. A faster procedure would be to sort large batches in account number sequence and sequentially match the transaction file and the account file.

9   Study the operational schedule and look for greater efficiency.

Operational schedules seem to grow on their own. They just evolve. Many times a group of technicians outside the operational management group can spot ways to rearrange the processing schedule to gain greater efficiency. For example, certain noncritical jobs can be run outside of the on-line day to increase the response time of the on-line functions.

INPUT AND OUTPUT PROCESSING

Many business data processing departments have a large and costly data entry section. Although in the future, voice recognition and other high technology innovations will reduce the traditional data entry function, key tape and key disk machines will be around for a long time. Even though data entry is being distributed to user departments, the basic function and basic problems of data entry will remain the same. Also, with the development of low cost microprocessor technology, these machines will develop more powerful editing and consolidation functions and will become even more valuable for certain large applications in the next few years. Data entry will still remain one of the largest sections in a company, and the audit team should spend some time evaluating its various difficulties and production concerns.

One common problem noted by data entry managers and supervisors, as well as by data entry personnel themselves, is lack of clarity of certain documents. A hard-to-read document can easily require twice the normal amount of time to enter into the system, and those documents are often the source of errors and misinterpretations. Even on-line editing is not the complete answer.

An occasional hard-to-read document is to be expected, but the audit team should look for specific divisions, sections, or even a particular clerk who may be responsible for many of such hard-to-read and hard-to-process documents. The audit team can point out such instances and recommend that DP and user group management work with the people who tend to produce those documents. Sometimes just a frank discussion with one person can reduce or even stop the problem with a resulting increase in the efficiency and productivity of the data entry group. Also, simply spreading this word around the company may significantly improve the quality of input forms and documents.

A second problem may be the arrangement of data on specific documents. As user requirements change, the original form designed by data processing may have been modified several times, but never redesigned. The audit team should study each important or commonly used form, including original documents, such as invoices or billing, and recommend which, if any, should be reevaluated for design errors.

A third source of difficulty in data entry is the timing of workloads. Data entry managers consistently complain that the typical weekly workload is unbalanced and causes a light load on one day and an impossible work schedule the next day. Although some of the cyclical, high-pressure aspects of data entry can never be eliminated, the audit team may find ways for the data entry group to function more evenly.

For example, a time-critical batch of input may depend upon regular company mail or delivery service to get from accounts payable to the data entry section. Special arrangements to move the documents as fast as possible may give an extra hour or so that was previously not available. Also, special, high-priority batches of input must be clearly marked and handled with special arrangements. Such clear markings and procedures will eliminate the ever popular answer, "But I didn't know it was that important!"

The audit team should examine the input procedures and operation for the data entry department, with consultation from user groups, and recommend any obvious solutions or suggest further study by management.

Output processing is another area in which an internal technical audit can recommend specific improvements to save paper and processing time. In almost all cases, of course, the recommendations will be that management or other teams study the specific situations and determine if it is possible to accomplish the recommended changes.

Possible improvements include considering the use of microfiche for large-volume reports, eliminating unnecessary copies of reports, increasing the print spacing from six to eight lines on stock preprinted forms, and studying preprinted forms to determine whether they should be redesigned. The audit team will generally work with the users and pose "what if" type questions. The buyers in a merchandising company, for example, may need to see a sample of an eight-line-per-inch report to determine if such a denser report (but with fewer pages) is useful as a working document.

An output problem common to some distributed systems is the lack of proper identification, such as time, date, originating source, and destination of the report. As DP environments become more complex, and information flows from location to location, all hardcopy reports should include the identification necessary to track down its source.

Companies installing on-line processing should evaluate printed reports and determine which are unnecessary or can be made unnecessary by installing additional on-line terminals or even more on-line reporting. Some organizations that have been on-line for years still produce printed, hard copy reports merely out of custom; they have never been examined for usefulness in the new operational environment.

DOCUMENTATION

Of all the aspects of data processing today, perhaps none causes more confusion and misunderstanding than the role of documentation in a business data processing shop. Documentation is always recommended by the professional staff, management, auditors, and the DP community in general. But how does an audit team evaluate the documentation in a busy production environment?

There is no easy answer. In the other audit areas, changes can be measured and logged precisely. Creating a backup tape at the same time as a master file in an inventory control update job may save thirty minutes a week run time. Spreading sortwork data sets among all devices can be shown to decrease run time an average of seven percent. But creating and maintaining documentation is one of those intangibles that even the experts have a hard time justifying from a strictly dollars and cents viewpoint.

The best approach for an audit team is to evaluate, in general terms, the state of internal documentation based upon a set of "best case" descriptions of data processing documentation. Few data processing installations can or will ever measure up to these proposed standards, but the audit team should still make the comparisons. It will at least provide the team with means to measure progress from year to year.

Assuming that data processing management does believe that internal systems and programming documentation is justified (and would like the internal audit team to evaluate such documentation), the team can use the following generalized standards for documentation.

1   Documentation must be created with a specific audience in mind. Documentation designed for a programmer will be different in tone and content from that designed for the accounts payable staff. Too often, the same documentation is distributed to different users, and each group is confused by sections intended for another group.

2   The best documentation is written by people with a clear, straightforward style.

A manual that reads like a COBOL or ASSEMBLER program is of little value and will probably never be used successfully, except by the one in 10 million people in the world who derives extreme joy from reading COBOL or ASSEMBLER programs. The other nine million, nine hundred, ninety-nine thousand plus people prefer to read manuals that look like *Reader's Digest*. Companies with sales, marketing, or even public relations departments can use those professionals to evaluate the current documentation and determine its readability.

3   Documentation must be available for immediate use by the entire professional staff.

Sometimes a project leader or manager may keep the only set of systems documentation in his or her office and tell his employees to "Feel free to borrow it anytime." However, most people are reluctant to intrude on closed-door meetings or break in when the project leader or manager appears busy. As a result, they fail to use the documentation. Better methods are to have documentation in a commonly accessible location, to distribute copies to offices, or to distribute copies to all staff members.

4   The users of documentation are the best judges of its quality and completeness.

Although management or the senior professional staff will usually decide on the organization and content of systems documentation, good, practical documentation is best evaluated and criticized by the actual users. A DP department which has simply presented a user with a set of manuals should not be surprised if they are ignored because they may be inadequate. The time to involve users is during the creation of the documentation.

5   Documentation must be updated, controlled, and distributed by one person.

Without a defined procedure for their updating, most documentation manuals will become obsolete and eventually useless. One person in the organization should assume responsibility for this procedure.

6   Documentation in general needs to be an ongoing, continual project.
Even if the inventory control system has not had a major change for several years, maintenance projects will have discovered important new information about that system that had not been previously documented. Some well-defined means should exist for adding this new information to the current documentation manuals, and the procedure itself should be well documented and easy to use.

7   For documentation to be of any value, it must be used by the professional staff.
Senior- and middle-level management should encourage the use and updating of documentation by their own example. The best documentation in the world will be useless if management does not encourage the professional staff to use it as a starting point for training, system maintenance, and project-development work.

Any audit of internal and external system documentation will be difficult because the DP profession still has not made documentation a standardized feature of systems and programming like languages or even system development techniques. However, a good internal audit should at least touch on all available internal and external systems documentation.

10

Managing the Trends

The technology of data processing is moving so fast and in so many directions that managers at all levels must periodically restructure their decisions to accommodate the new developments. It is hard to know whether a change indicates a definite trend or simply a buzzword or media promotion. The explosion in information publications has complicated the issue further, as more writers jump on the bandwagon to push their own personal theories and attitudes. If people are the single most complicated aspect of data processing to successfully manage, surely the rapidly changing hardware and software technology must be the second most frustrating area to control. Change by its very nature is a process that must be carefully analyzed and controlled by farsighted management, or it will wind up controlling the managers with disastrous results.

Some trends in computer technology are obvious and require little discussion. For example, the decreasing cost of microprocessors has created microcomputers that not only rival the mainframes of 15 years ago, but are also rapidly becoming an integral part of many large corporations. The issue is not the specific technological trend but rather the way in which these new technologies are handled. No trend is a cure-all or solution to the problems of the world—in fact, every new development in hardware or software technology requires the best efforts of technological managers to solve the problems the new developments will bring. Only by careful, businesslike analysis, can the data processing executives of the 1980s hope to control the genies that have been unleashed in the engineering laboratories.

DISTRIBUTED PROCESSING: THE ANSWER TO WHAT QUESTION?

The first problem with distributed data processing—and the reason it can cause such great controversy—is that most organizations have seized on the distributed approach as the answer to all their problems. The second problem with distributed data processing is that managers and executives fail to understand the basic reasons for its initial marketing successes and are ignorant of the basic, underlying problems, which will usually lead to frustration, dissatisfaction, and costly management blunders.

Distributed processing in its original form was a good solution in search of a problem, and the DP world in the late 1970s had a wide variety of problems to solve. Reports from batch applications were consistently late, and user requests to upgrade batch applications were often ignored. On-line interactive processing—once thought to be its own ultimate answer to the problems of the world—did boost productivity and make possible a new range of business applications, but it also created its own unique set of conditions. Some on-line systems took years to develop and were partially obsolete by the time they were put into production. Others required so much additional CPU power that some lucky hardware vendors found an instant goldmine. Still other applications took so many highly skilled programmers to maintain or change that the true cost of on-line processing increased dangerously close to the "unjustifiable level." Although a significant number of on-line application systems did come through for the user with powerful interactive processing, the DP management team still faced their own surprises and frustrations.

At the same time, the cost of computer processors dropped dramatically, and hardware vendors immediately proposed minicomputers as the answer to deficiencies in business and scientific application systems. Data processing management, user management, and even senior company executives looked to the new buzzword of distributed processing to relieve the frustrations associated with the older centralized systems. No, it wasn't the detailed cost and benefits analysis covering 15 typed pages that convinced everyone of the practicality of DDP. It wasn't a five-hour marathon discussion with senior company executives on the philosophical advantages of user control of data that persuaded the controller to authorize the purchase of a minicomputer for the Boston plant. Most companies never prepared a 15-page cost and benefits analysis, and most corporate controllers were lucky to give a DP manager 20 minutes of their time every month.

The plant manager and the controller could care less who actually controls the data, if they even understood the issues involved. They chose the distributed approach because it could reduce their personal frustration by apparently solving specific and measurable problems. If the computer was in the accounting department, wouldn't the accounting reports come out faster and better? That question may be laughable to the DP technicians, but it was deadly serious to the user management who pressed for its own hardware and to the company executives who reluctantly approved those requests.

The bottom line of the original push for DDP was that users wanted a method to correct deficiencies with the centralized system, and to evaluate, select, and manage this distributed function successfully, the smart manager will approach the entire issue as "solutions" rather than buzzwords. What specifically does the accounting or plant manager want out of his or her proposed distributed system? "Better service" is not acceptable from a business standpoint, and neither is a rapid fire collection of fascinating but meaningless buzzwords straight from a hardware marketing representative. Distributed processing must be justified by concrete, measurable, and well-defined objectives, not by theoretical platitudes that sound great over a drink but fail miserably when subjected to a business evaluation. Some valid justifications for a DDP system are:

1   Reducing response time of the on-line transactions from six seconds to three.

2   Extending the hours of operation to match the requirements of
    the operating unit.
3   Producing the daily sales summary report three hours earlier.
4   Providing interactive capabilities that the central system does not
    possess.
5   Producing an entirely new custom-made system to meet a spe-
    cific need.

In each example, the cost per executable instruction of minicomputers, as opposed to that of large mainframes, was irrelevant, and
the hotly debated question of centralized versus decentralized control
of data was not important. The true issues of DDP can only be discussed if data processing management is willing to face the reason for
favoring the distributed approach: *Users perceive they can manage
problem areas and bypass the data processing department with distributed processing.* Data processing technical and management
personnel must document accurately each proposed solution to a
specific problem from the user's viewpoint. Only when senior DP executives understand which problems the users expect to be solved
can they ever hope to correctly design a distributed system. It is a
serious error for the DP management team to approve a $200,000
distributed system only to discover that the new hardware and software do not satisfy the frustrated users. The plant manager may not
really understand what he or she expects out of a distributed data
processing system, but it is the job of the DP managers to help the
plant manager define those expectations in measurable terms.
Measurable means definable and objective, not subjective or emo-
tional. Giving control over data elements to a user is an interesting,
promising, and inspiring concept in the trade journals, but it is usually not worth $200,000.
   Mini- and microcomputer systems can obviously be cost effective
solutions to certain business problems and can increase the productivity and reliability of the corporate data processing organizations,
but only when they are used in a well-conceived situation and all
parties know exactly what to expect. But in reality, many DDP systems are installed with little or no data processing staff involvement,
or are purchased with little management control. Under those conditions, a DDP site can sometimes become an expensive liability and

cause "distributed headaches," which are every bit as painful as the more traditional centralized headaches.

The dangers of DDP can be minimized if data processing management takes an active role. Many of the managers who complain that users go over their heads have only themselves to blame. Centralized DP managers have too often looked upon distributed data processing as a threat to their personal empire and have consequently alienated potential DDP users. These users then turn away from potentially valuable help.

Centralized DP management rarely controls the distributed data processing decisions in companies where the prime motivator for DDP is simply a large group of frustrated users who want better service. The only reasonable approach to minimizing the serious potential problems in those organizations is for DP centralized management to admit the generalized dissatisfaction and actively help the users. Distributed processing is a long-term trend that cannot be avoided, ignored, or dismissed, and a DP management team which does try to ignore a DDP movement will lose in the end. The specific DDP experiment in question may indeed fail, and the users may retire to lick their wounds, but the bad feelings generated during the failure will come back to haunt the DP managers and the entire company. Smart managers will ignore their egos and actually help a user group trying to build their own distributed system.

Even with the positive cooperation and assistance of DP technicians and managers, a distributed data processing system can flounder unless the entire evaluation team approaches the proposed DDP system from a business viewpoint and asks the right questions at the right time. It may be difficult to get past the slick marketing jargon and the thrill of having hands-on computer capability, but these business questions must be answered.

The first step is to have the users define the proposed benefits from a distributed system in terms of written functional specifications. As many organizations have discovered, users will be disappointed and frustrated unless they have measurable, concrete reasons for a decentralized processing scheme.

The second potential problem area is that many users fail to recognize the manual human efforts needed to operate any computer. Mini- and microcomputers are far less dependent on full-time computer operators than large mainframes, but someone still must occasionally power up the system, change a disk pack, perform shutdown procedures, change paper in the printer, do basic diagnostics if needed, and in general make sure the hardware is functioning properly. Mini- and microcomputers vary significantly in the degree of human intervention necessary: A simple system with basic on-line processing and one permanently sealed disk will require far less attention than a mini with removable disk packs and a printer. The user must know in advance the manual support needed in his or her proposed system and should designate one individual (and a backup) to perform those tasks.

Another frequently overlooked consideration is the hardware reliability and corresponding maintenance procedures. A CPU might have an impressive mean-time-between-failure (MTBF), but it means nothing when the power goes off during an electrical storm, or the printer breaks, or the janitor bumps into the disk controller. Users must be prepared, with documented procedures, for interruptions in their distributed system. Vendor representatives often praise the reliability of minicomputer systems and frequently point out that distributed applications will continue running even when the central computer is down for hardware, software, or maintenance reasons. They seldom tell potential users, however, that the central computer will be running when their own distributed system is down for hardware, software, or maintenance reasons.

If hardware reliability is the prime concern for the particular application, the evaluation should consider the *network approach*, or *building-block concept,* that connects multiple minicomputers so that when one fails the other can temporarily share the processing load. Obviously, certain types of hardware problems in the lines connecting the CPUs may still cause application system failure, but such a network gives more up time and reliability than the classic single CPU distributed system. In some situations a building block architecture is a better choice, and it should always be considered.

Every distributed installation needs a disaster plan just as badly as a large centralized installation that serves thousands of on-line terminals. What will the order entry department do when their minicomputer is down for three hours? Is there a backup procedure that will allow phone and telex orders to be recorded for later entry, or will the order entry staff be forced to tell customers to call back? If the mini in the warehouse that controls the on-line receiving function breaks down, how will the receiving dock manager handle shipping and distribution? Obviously, he or she cannot send trucks back and the 30-member staff home, but he or she must have a combination of forms, procedures, and trained people ready to go back to a manual procedure to keep both the system and company in operation. The only time to develop a disaster plan for a DDP site is before the disaster or problem actually happens.

Technical problems must be adequately planned for. A hardware vendor trying to sell a turnkey minicomputer system to the accounting manager may not mention that disk crashes do occasionally occur, that power surges can sometimes damage unprotected electronic circuits, or that the new clerk may accidentally select the monthly general ledger update when he or she should have started the weekly reporting cycle. What happens when the disk pack containing the general ledger chart of accounts file is damaged? Does the accounting manager know how to recover from a backup disk? Are there any backup procedures or files? Does anyone in the accounting department truly understand that recovery plans are an absolute necessity? If not, it is the job of the data processing advisory team to teach them.

A final danger in the rush to implement a DDP site is that users who are not accustomed to managing a computer will not look at the true expense of any piece of hardware. Too often a salesperson will propose a one-price package deal that is supposedly "everything" the accounting or sales processing department will need to implement a complete distributed system. Marketing and sales people, however, usually fail to mention the ongoing and startup costs that are always associated with hardware. Maintenance contracts can sometimes run 15 percent or more of the yearly lease payment, and this may not include replacement of certain mechanical parts that wear out or become defective. Whereas a totally on-line interactive-only system will have very low ongoing expenses, other mini and microcomputer systems will require paper and ribbons for the printer, additional disk packs or diskettes, longer cables for moving the terminals, and storage equipment. Many distributed data processing managers are unprepared for the initial expense of purchasing storage cabinets. Proper filing equipment and antisurge protectors are expenses that only experienced DP managers can predict. Distributed data processing hardware involves far more than the purchase order for the original computer system, and any company planning for DDP must be aware of those expensive needs.

USER INVOLVEMENT: MORE THAN A PHRASE

The watchword for the 1980s and beyond is *user involvement*. The end users will be involved in every aspect of data processing, including designing the original system, developing the modules, and testing the final results.

Interestingly enough, the demand for end user involvement came from factors which operated during the late 1960s and 1970s. The first factor was a strong feeling that data processing technology was so complicated that accountants, marketing managers, budget planning experts, and corporate presidents could not possibly understand it. As a result, companies consistently found that computerized applications did not meet the basic needs of the users. It appeared that the technical wizards who could magically get the computer to print payroll checks were themselves mere mortals when it came to understanding the aging process of an accounts receivable distribution or the pricing intricacies of contract catalog pricing calculations. The business world finally realized that computer experts were not expert in everything, and that the end users could not be ignored until the final implementation date.

The second factor that demanded end user involvement was the rising cost of complicated business application systems. In the 1960s, two programmers may have created a basic working payroll system in 10 weeks, but in the 1980s, a complex application project can now require 10 or 20 expensive systems analysts and programmers. The hardware cost per CPU cycle dropped dramatically, but the cost in development time rose just as dramatically. Corporate controllers could no longer accept a complaint by the accounting manager that the new general ledger system was nice but made it almost impossible to reverse a duplicate entry—a problem which usually occurred 10 times a week. Such a costly system certainly had to satisfy the people who would use it.

A third factor which encouraged user involvement was the consideration that purchased software packages were a valid alternative to in-house development. Once corporate-level managers got over the shock of evaluating high-priced application software by comparing a one-time expense to the true cost of developing an in-house system (usually by multiplying the data processing managers' estimate by a factor of five), many executives finally realized the potential benefits. Good software packages were a known quantity; they were seldom custom tailored to an organization, but with modifications could be made satisfactory. The selection of a proper software application system required experts not only from the data processing section but also from the end user groups. Accounting people may not have known one operating system from another, but they definitely know the requirements for a good chart-of-accounts structure. Payroll managers may have never seen a tape or a disk pack but, they have definite ideas on the need for immediate inquiries on the payroll file. Without heavy and continuous end user involvement, companies frequently purchased inadequate application packages.

If the trend toward direct user involvement is to be successful, data processing managers should take the lead in developing a planned, realistic approach to working with users. Too often a combined team of DP staff and users will sit at a conference table with all the cooperation of two nine-year-old boys fighting over a baseball bat. The children spend more time arguing over who should have the bat first than they do playing, and the DP/user team spends more time jockeying for political power and pointing out each other's ignorance than it does in jointly solving a problem or making a valid recommendation. In the decade of the 1980s, such unbusinesslike behavior cannot be tolerated. The stakes of economic survival and profitability are now too high to allow individuals or groups to play ego games inside the organization.

Egoless managers are in a perfect position to break the cycle of disagreement and mistrust which seems to develop whenever data processing staff and users get together. Management-level personnel who can put aside their own ego needs and desire for power, influence, and money can rise above the situation and direct the joint DP-user task force toward productivity instead of frustration.

Several very simple steps can help insure such a team approach.

First, nontechnical users must be educated in basic DP concepts, such as disk versus tape operations, data base as opposed to conventional file organizations, and in-house development versus purchased packages. The nature of the educational process will depend on the situation and circumstances of the organization and the specific project. Most DP managers would be astounded at the lack of basic conceptual understanding that most nontechnical users possess but are afraid to admit publicly. Often this lack of understanding is a direct cause of tension and resentment from users who are continually baffled by data processing terminology and concepts. The bottom-line advice for DP managers who are involved in heavy user interface is to make sure that all basic technical concepts are well understood by the non-technical people.

A second principle is to verify that all data processing personnel involved in a design or evaluation project with users have a basic understanding of the application in question. Just as many DP managers are surprised by the lack of basic computer knowledge found in many nontechnical users, other managers are equally surprised at the lack of communication caused by DP personnel who have absolutely no idea what the users are talking about. Even experienced DP managers who have come up through the ranks fail to realize that both programmer/analysts and system analysts may lack a working knowledge of a given application system. A system analyst who has developed inventory control systems for a retail company may know the principles of inventory management but may have serious misconceptions about the inventory control philosophy of a manufacturing company. Even a competent programmer/analyst who has worked extensively with payroll systems in other companies may not understand the payroll procedures in the new organization. Misconceptions may even be worse than complete ignorance. In order for data processing managers or senior technicians to interact successfully with users, they must make a concentrated effort to learn the basics of the company and the individual application. Such an effort takes time and management support, but it is an absolute business necessity, and organizations which fail to make such an effort eventually pay the price in terms of incorrect system designs and frustrated users.

One obvious but frequently overlooked technique to educate the DP staff in a specific application is to arrange for selected individuals to spend a morning or afternoon with a user. Watching a retail buyer using inventory control reports to increase his or her margin or following an accounting manager trying to close a month-end update is an interesting and educational experience. If approached in a positive manner, most users would be willing to participate in such a program.

A final way to educate the DP professional staff is to actually have them use the input and output procedures, such as data entry forms and CRT input screens. There is a significant difference between watching an order entry clerk enter data to inquire about a back order and spending 15 minutes at a terminal trying to use the on-line inquiry system. There is no substitute for actually experiencing how the application system works. On the output side, many programmer/analysts, system analysts, and DP managers have never even seen the reports they are responsible for. But seeing a report or output screen is only half the battle; DP professionals and managers must read and use the output before they can truly understand the user's point of view.

Once the DP staff and users have been cross-trained to some degree, or are at least participating in such a program, the data processing managers in the group should take the lead by planning the entire task around a formalized project management approach. The degree of formalization depends on the length, complexity, and importance of the task or project, but the data processing section usually has people with project management experience and can recommend the most appropriate management approach. Under no circumstances should a large user and DP team sit down at a conference table without a written agenda and mutually understood goals. While unstructured meetings among several people to help plan the approach and agenda will naturally take place, the more formalized restrictions should always apply when four or more interdepartment people attend a scheduled meeting. Two or three managers sitting down to "blue sky" ways to approach a proposed on-line credit verification system will not need a written agenda, but when the seven-member development team has their first formal meeting, they will need a written agenda. Interdepartmental meetings are too tricky and too expensive to not manage properly.

THE RULE OF NINE MONTHS

People dislike waiting. Sick people don't like sitting around in waiting rooms until the doctor finally shows up. Teenagers don't like getting to a rock concert four hours early just to find a good seat. Parents don't care to sit around in the family station wagon waiting for their son to get out of basketball practice. And the users of a computerized application don't like waiting years for something they need.

This impatience has combined with a disturbing and frustrating trend in data processing that became more common in the late 1970s. Many organizations were stunned and angered to discover that the systems which took one, two, or even three years to develop were obsolete by the time they were finally put in production. These applications may have indeed met the original design specification, but by the time they were complete, the user requirements, company policy, business environment, or the users themselves had changed. The big, expensive development project that was designed to put in an on-line accounts receivable system did not do a satisfactory job. The term frequently heard in data processing offices and corporate boardrooms was, "Yes, it works, but . . . ." Users were not satisfied because in many cases they were not the same users who had helped with the design requirements. Changing business conditions or a new company organization may have nullified some of the original design criteria. And the actual working system may have missed certain key functions that every accounts receivable manager knows but somehow did not filter down by osmosis to the programmers who wrote the master update modules. After the famous, "Yes, it works, but . . . ." the next key phrase became, "I thought it was supposed to . . . ." The system was not only late, but it was also incomplete. Users were not completely satisfied and neither were the data processing professionals who worked nights and weekends trying to finish a project that had already gone on one year past the original deadline.

In the 1980s, the rapidly changing technology, an unsettled business environment, and changing market conditions will prevent companies from planning projects which extend several years into the future. The high cost of DP development projects—whether creating an in-house system or modifying a purchased application package—makes it impractical to invest a large amount of money in people and resources when the return will be years in the future. Besides, many business people, from programmer/analysts to corporate officers, now realize that an application system planned for three years in the future may not be right when it is finally ready. It is simply too hard to predict the business environment three years ahead in many organizations. The problem is not necessarily one of poor planning, substandard design, and inadequate management, but rather a situation where the business world can change so fast that long-term specific application system planning is no longer reliable.

One approach is the "rule of nine months." If a data processing development project cannot furnish the user with measurable results in nine months or less, the project should not be undertaken. There will be some exceptions, but the goal of data processing management in the 1980s should be to schedule a project within nine months. That is, the user should be able to use some portion of the new application within that time period or at least see significant progress.

If nature can produce a human being in that time, there are rarely valid reasons why data processing managers cannot develop a working application subset for a general ledger system in the same amount of time. The subset may not be complete or perfect, but it should serve a useful purpose and give the company back some of its investment.

Too often in both business and scientific data processing the management philosophy is to follow the "rule of two years"—the same amount of time nature requires to produce an elephant. Wise data processing managers should recognize that whereas the final product of a nine-month development cycle may require clean-up activities including an occasional change in diapers, the clean up of a two-year development project will require a shovel and rubber boots.

OUTSIDE APPLICATION PACKAGES:
TO BUY OR NOT TO BUY

The rising costs of in-house development projects have forced harried data processing managers to consider buying ready-made application systems. On the surface, this appears to be a logical solution, and as a result, the application software industry grew rapidly during the 1970s. In the early 1970s companies discovered that a purchased payroll package could successfully replace a manual or an obsolete in-house system. In the late 1970s they discovered several well-designed accounting systems that could be installed fairly easily and even worked successfully the first time! As more and more organizations compared the feasibility of an in-house development project with that of a canned outside system, the computer software industry exploded with new packaged systems.

The trend for the 1980s is clear. Any DP management team considering replacing the so-called "bread and butter" systems—payroll, accounts payable, accounts receivable, and general ledger—should look first to outside packages and then to possible in-house development. Few data processing installations have the on-board expertise to create such a complex system from scratch, and even fewer can afford the usually greater development cost. A "bread and butter" application that has a reasonable fit to the internal procedure in a company will usually win an honest side-by-side cost comparison of packages and internal development projects. One must consider the scarcity of trained professional talent; even if a company did want to develop an in-house accounts payable system, could they afford to commit most of their programming staff to that one project? Would it not be better to buy a generalized accounts payable system, adapt the internal company procedures to meet the requirements of the new system, and use the programming staff to create a specialized budget planning system. Critically short staffing situations in many organizations are increasing the already solid business value of buying canned application systems.

Another trend that began seriously in the late 1970s was that some software companies—even the small organizations—plunged into areas that were formerly reserved for in-house development. End users could now buy complete applications such as order entry, inventory control, credit management, and fixed asset accounting systems. Other software companies targeted specific industries, such as the manufacturing or wholesale distribution industries, and provided an integrated set of application systems. Suddenly the decision to buy or not to buy became more complicated and required a special combination of business and technical skills that most DP managers did not possess. Too many decisions were based on hunches, guesses, or an outright flip of a coin, and some of those decisions even cost a few unlucky DP managers their jobs.

Choosing between specialized packages is a difficult matter and must be approached scientifically and with a concern for business criteria. It is impossible to make the ultimate decision between buying a package and writing the application in-house unless the DP and user team have previously picked the best available software product. Unfortunately, some evaluation teams merely pick one canned system at random and use that single package to help make their "buy or not to buy" decision. Such a short-cut can be dangerous, especially with the complex factors that now enter into such a decision in the 1980s.

Buying a software package is just as risky as buying a used car from a fast-talking salesperson wearing a loud plaid sport jacket and smoking a foul-smelling cigar. The bad car may strand the buyer in the middle of nowhere on a dark, stormy night, and the wrong software package may do the same thing to an unsuspecting data processing manager.

There are some very simple ways for data processing management to deal with the increasing trend toward software packages and avoid the horror stories detailed in the trade press.

First, DP managers must have the serious commitment of both company management and the user management team to spend the time and money necessary to properly make the "buy or develop" decision. Users must plan on devoting large blocks of their time to help the data processing professionals study the capabilities and limitations of each package. If a busy accounting manager tells the controller that he or she would be happy to spend any time necessary to help evaluate general ledger systems, the data processing manager may legitimately ask whether the accounting manager has delegated any of his or her normal responsibilities. Users may not quite realize the large amounts of uninterrupted time that package software evaluation requires. It is the responsibility of data processing to make sure all users are aware of this fact. Senior company management should allocate up to several thousand dollars for trips to observe the proposed software package in use. An order entry manager can memorize every product brochure and user documentation manual for a specific application system but will never truly conceptualize the operating characteristics of the system until he or she sees it working. The printed word is a great invention, but it cannot totally replace a real live person watching a real live system processing real live data. Those who do not understand this concept are ignoring the limitations of the human mind.

Second, the evaluation team must realize that packaged software systems are sometimes cost justified only if the user departments are willing to modify their internal operating procedures. Rarely will a company find a package that precisely fits their needs, and in many cases the company will have to give up some current features in order to get the immediate benefits of a canned application system. Although packages have become more flexible and powerful during the past few years and have given users more options to choose from, the user managers must understand at the start that some changes are inevitable. There is rarely a perfect fit for a software application package. The only question is "how much" and "what." If the user managers take the attitude that no changes are possible and if management supports their position, the evaluation team is starting the project with two outs and two strikes in the ninth inning. There is always the chance of a home run or of locating a package that will fit the company perfectly, but the odds are against it. The best management policy is to make sure that both users and company executives know the score before the game ends in a loss.

Third, the senior technicians and managers involved in the project should look beyond the sales pitch and thoroughly examine the limitations of the package. In buying software—or even hardware—the key factors may be those things the package will *not* do, and discovering those potential problems is no easy matter. Vacuum cleaner salespeople rarely demonstrate the type of dirt their machines will *not* pick up. Application package marketing people will emphasize the positive features of their system but will seldom point out those aspects of a company's business the package cannot handle successfully.

The accounts payable manager may be impressed by a list of the automatic functions triggered when the accounting period closes, but the data processing manager should encourage him or her to ask what will happen when the accounting periods must be reopened to correct a mistake. The inventory control system may have a very impressive ten-digit store number, but can it handle the required consolidated store numbering scheme? The only way to get such information is to approach the marketing people with the goal of discovering limitations as they relate to the individual company and user department. Such a seemingly negative approach can often give surprisingly positive results because the evaluation team will have a more realistic and rational basis for making their final recommendations. Surprises are great for a birthday party but are not appropriate when implementing a $50,000 accounts payable system.

Since purchased application systems are becoming more common in most organizations, managers at all levels need to familiarize themselves with the scope and power of these packages by reading the trade journals and newspapers as well as by reading specific product brochures. Successful data processing managers of the 1980s will already be familiar with the software product industry before the specific need arises.

THE SEARCH FOR ALTERNATIVES

The goal of data processing today is to provide high-quality DP services for the lowest cost. Distributed data processing and purchased application packages are only two of the alternatives. In the 1980s, both data processing executives and senior management must continually examine the new hardware and software technology for new ways of improving their operation.

It is just as dangerous to blindly accept the challenge of the new technologies as it is to try to ignore new developments. The difficulty lies in separating the glamour of new hardware and software options from their true business value. For example, distributed processing is a useful architectural trend, but does it make good business sense for the individual company and the individual application, or do some managers recommend it because it is almost a fad? Is a data base machine a worthwhile investment, or would the data processing installation be farther ahead using those same funds to upgrade the main CPU? Is light fiber optics a realistic alternative for a local network, or would a standard telephone line actually serve the same purpose? It is both necessary and exciting to follow the trends in data processing as they develop and affect people across the world, but it is just as important to critically evaluate such trends from a business standpoint. When data processing managers learn to stop thinking like technicians and start thinking like business people, they will become true managers and take their rightful place in the organization.

11

Managing the Hardware

In all but a few lucky companies, data processing managers control the hardware of their installation by the old-fashioned "management by crisis" technique. The hardware configuration in a computer center is usually ignored until the accounting manager complains to the senior vice-president that he or she can no longer live with 10-second-response time for the general ledger edit transactions, or the production manager announces that warehouse documents are late for the fifth time in a month. Only then will some DP managers look upon the CPU, the I/O channels, and the peripherals as business resources which must be properly managed *before* they become a matter of crisis. If DP managers are surprised when called into the senior vice-president's office to hear complaints of poor response time and poor service to the users, they have only themselves to blame.

Interestingly enough, the large installations that recognize the importance of hardware often have full-time performance analysts with the responsibility of monitoring computer capacity and matching it to the demands of the users. But even these organizations can be caught by surprise, because data processing management has consistently failed to communicate important issues in terms that nontechnicians can understand. Senior management has consequently ignored the recommendations of DP management teams, and the hardware and software have been relegated to the "MBC" (management by crisis) approach. The organization finally reacts when there is no choice. The bottom line advice for data processing managers is to make performance evaluations understandable. *If the department secretary cannot understand the report, the board of directors may not understand either.*

The most obvious solution is to locate and hire a top-notch computer performance analyst to continually monitor the hardware and software capabilities of the installation as they relate to the application systems. However, even the best performance analyst who remains locked in his or her office and memorizes detailed reports from hardware and software monitors will do a poor job unless he or she can match his or her analyses to the actual application systems. The truly expert performance analysts know the applications and jobstreams almost as well as they understand channel programs and hardware monitoring reports. Such people can be developed through proper management direction, and most large installations can easily justify hiring one if they make hardware decisions more than once a year.

Another solution which is less costly but can be equally effective is to start a program of continuous performance measurement, using the current senior technical and managerial staff. For too long DP managers have tried to justify additional or improved hardware with the vague justification of "The computer is now overloaded" or "We need more disk space." When pressed for more details, the manager might show the vice-president a mysterious and wonderous chart of EXCP's and CPU utilization statistics, but the data processing management team was rarely involved in continuous performance measurement and evaluation. There were plenty of other crises to worry about, and the hardware could be ignored until it too became a matter of crisis. With the rapidly changing technology and the unsettled business conditions in the 1980s, DP managers can no longer afford to allow the hardware aspect of their jobs to manage them.

WHAT IS PERFORMANCE?

The performance in a computer center can be measured in everything from the number of jobs processed each day to the response time for an item inquiry transaction to the number of lines printed each month. If 10 people in a committee try to select the best single measure of data center performance, they will inevitably come up with 11 opinions. Every proposed measure has some validity and can be used to more or less evaluate individual aspects of total computer processing. But when looking at a computer installation from a true business perspective and considering the ultimate purpose of most computer centers, the best measure of data center performance is ultimately user satisfaction. In simple terms, if the users are performing their jobs satisfactorily using computer output, the data center's performance is acceptable. If the users are not satisfied and consequently not able to do their jobs, the performance of the computer is not acceptable. User satisfaction is unfortunately a subjective measure, but it is still the ultimate judgment of success or failure. It can be made somewhat less subjective, however, if data processing managers approach the issue in a logical and scientific manner.

The most obvious, and most overlooked, requirement of a data center performance evaluation project is to document the performance standards from the user's point of view. Customers judge data processing by comparing their input with the output in the form of a printed report, an answer to a question, or an output screen on a CRT. A batch of general ledger transactions may be delivered to the data entry section, and four hours later the edit report is handed to the accounting clerk. The accounting manager sees a four-hour turnaround time although the actual computer processing may have taken two minutes. Only total job or task turnaround is valid when documenting performance standards from a business viewpoint.

Any written standard should be expressed in terms of level of service. That is, the DP manager may commit to a three-hour turnaround for accounting edit batches 98 percent of the time. In the real world of data processing there will be some legitimate circumstances when it is impossible to provide good or even reasonable service due to hardware, software, or even staffing problems. It is unrealistic to deny that such situations ever happen, and it is always better to plan for such events rather than be surprised when they do occur.

Standards should be arranged to allow for differences in actual computer hardware processing. An inquiry on an open purchase order may require comparatively few resources and could be answered in only two seconds, whereas an update transaction to calculate a pricing discount may take an average of seven seconds. It is wrong to expect all on-line transactions to be processed in the same amount of time, and it is equally wrong to demand that all transactions have the same response time during a 24-hour day. One way to quantify such variable activities is to select several of the more common transactions and establish individual standards for each appropriate to specific times of the on-line day. For example, a valid and easily measured standard is to expect that 98 percent of all item inquiry transactions will be processed within three seconds if triggered between 9:00 A.M. and 10:00 A.M. Conversely, an open order addition to an existing purchase order could take a maximum of seven seconds when processed during the same time period. A batch of accounts payable transactions which have less than 2,000 lines could be keypunched, processed, and the report given to the edit clerk within three hours, except on a month-end week, 95 percent of the time. Any standard must be specific enough to be measured, but general enough to take into account the workings of the data processing section.

Performance standards must consider the scheduling coordination between the data processing section and the individual user sections. If a batch balance total must be verified before the operations section can begin their seven-hour weekly update run, how long should the verification take, and what will be the effect if it is delayed? If the accounting people take two hours to balance the edit reports instead of 30 minutes, is data processing still required to finish the update and reporting by the scheduled time? The answer should be settled in writing when the standards are originally developed and not saved for the traditional battles between data processing and user management. The user groups do have a strong responsibility to follow procedures and schedules which allow the data processing section to meet their end of the bargain. Although batch type systems, such as accounts payable or payroll updates, are the most obvious examples of user responsibility, even many on-line applications require the users to input all necessary transactions by specific time periods. Too often, a frustrated user manager will ask the DP director to extend the on-line processing hours. This results in delays of the next morning's batch production and ultimately appears to be a failure of the data processing organization. Helping users by any reasonable means should be a trademark of a good DP manager, but everyone involved should be realistic enough to know the true price of any special assistance. A manager left holding the bag is usually a manager who did not consider the ultimate effects of his or her decisions. Such considerations must be an integral part of every set of published performance standards.

Written standards should be carefully evaluated by a joint team of experienced DP and user managers, and reviewed by the appropriate senior staff. By the very nature of their jobs, managers and directors should not be involved with the detailed production situation in a computer center and should allow the experienced staff to use their own judgment to catch potential problem areas before they become real problems. Many times a programmer, system analyst, or user can point out exceptional situations to proposed standards that have been missed by the managers creating those guidelines.

The second step in measuring that elusive goal of "user satisfaction" is to develop a method of regularly comparing actual computer center performance to the official published standards. Managers who wait until the complaints start pouring in before they finally decide to investigate the situation are too late; continuous performance evaluation should be as much a part of a well-run data processing organization as continuous people evaluation. Fortunately, since the DP management team should have written guidelines to help measure the operational performance, evaluating data center performance should be much easier than evaluating people.

A frequent objection to continual performance monitoring is that data processing people are too busy to complete the paperwork usually associated with performance measurement. This frequently stated objection should be rejected for two reasons. First, without adequate performance measurement, data processing managers with hardware and operational responsibility cannot do their jobs effectively. Performance measurement is a very important path to sound operational management; one cannot readily manage what one does not recognize. Second, monitoring the general operational performance of a data center does not have to become a nightmare of forms, memos, and charts that bury an already overworked data center staff in more paper. With a little ingenuity and planning, an operational management group can develop simple ideas which will automatically produce the raw data necessary for an effective performance evaluation program. Even keeping the raw information in the back of a file cabinet and never looking at it is still preferable to not having such facts in the first place. Experienced managers learn from hard experience that they never know when they may be summoned by senior management to justify their performance and the performance of their entire section or division.

An "output control log" can be a simple way to track the performance of batch type jobs. If a given batch of input must flow through five work stations before it is completed, the control log needs a column for the job name or number, a space for the date, and five columns representing each stage of a batch being processed. The DP or user staff member taking responsibility for each processing step should write his or her initials and time in the appropriate column. If the batch control log is made a standard requirement for all employees, data processing management will eventually have the raw data necessary to locate specific problem areas and to monitor actual turnaround time. Any data processing manager who does not periodically gather this type of turnaround data is leaving himself open to unjustified criticism. It is unrealistic to assume that because there are no current complaints from the user groups the entire data collection process is unnecessary.

Special requests which come in by phone should be logged on a special form for that purpose with the date, time, and person's initials. The all-too-common practice of allowing a request to be passed verbally may work satisfactorily most of the time, but the exceptions and the problems caused by verbal misunderstandings will cost more in management time and user dissatisfaction than the price of requiring staff members to transmit action requests in writing. Again, the monitoring procedure should not be difficult for the people involved. For example, if a data center had 10 types of frequent requests, the phone crew could develop a checklist form that would allow the phone person merely to check the appropriate request rather than write a description every time. The people doing the actual work should be responsible for creating forms and procedures that will make the tracking process as simple and efficient as possible while still facilitating the gathering of necessary raw information.

Jobs submitted via a remote job entry terminal or from a computer-to-computer network usually have no manual intervention and must be monitored by a system-operated job accounting package. Although most installations use job accounting systems as a chargeback or cost control mechanism, some of the more sophisticated packages can track job submittal and execution times.

Turnaround statistics will eventually be summarized for both operational and user managers, but the format of a summary should be determined by the managers who are to use the report. Instead of having a programmer or performance analyst propose a format, the end users should define their requirements on paper and then allow someone else to develop the report.

PERFORMANCE MEASUREMENT IN REAL TERMS

Although user satisfaction is the ultimate proof of performance of any given system, certain key indicators can provide the factual information necessary to verify those value judgments. In addition, these measures can discover trends and highlight future problems before they adversely affect the production systems. Experienced performance analysts have found that no one single indicator or measure is valid enough to judge the total performance of a data center; rather, selected combinations of these events can provide data processing management with enough understandable measures to demonstrate capacity and performance problems to nontechnical managers. The selection of these indicators can and will change whenever the data center significantly modifies its software or application architecture. Enhanced operating software, for example, will usually provide more accurate job accounting or monitoring functions than a more primitive operating system.

In practice, many of the measures finally chosen will be determined in large part by the job accounting statistics provided by the current data center software, or by facts which are available from users, data center employees, or current operating reports. A management team may prefer some statistics which are simply not available or would require significant expenditures in terms of new software or extra human effort. In most organizations the staff involved in a performance measurement project must work with existing indicators which are present or which can be made available with a minimum of cost.

One obvious measure is the total number of batch jobs put through

a system in a specified time frame. Although transaction-oriented installations view batch processing as a minor part of their total workload, many such data centers actually devote just as much computer
capacity to batch processing as to the more interesting and modern
on-line functions. Contrary to popular opinion, batch processing is
alive and well in most computer centers and cannot be ignored just
because management prefers to concentrate on the more glamorous
and exciting on-line updating and reporting activity. Banks, for example, may use the on-line inquiry and update functions heavily during
the on-line day but will still run large batch update applications at
night. The number of batch jobs is still, therefore, an indicator of
total output from almost any hardware configuration; the exceptions
are those CPUs which are totally dedicated to on-line interactive
processing.

Like many other indicators, the number of jobs processed during a
day means very little by itself. A shop which processes 5000 jobs
does not necessarily require more hardware resources than a shop
which runs only 500 jobs in the same time period. Four thousand,
nine hundred and ninety-nine of those 5000 jobs may be simple batch
item inquiries which take one-tenth of a second. The actual number
is almost meaningless, but the trend of those numbers can be significant, especially when that trend is combined with the trends from
other indicators.

The number of jobs in each time period should be plotted on graph
paper to be visually useful, with the time scale set up to handle several
references. For example, there should be one chart each for a week, a
calendar month, a calendar year, and for those organizations which
use accounting periods, another set which matches production cycles.
The calendar graphs will illustrate the trends which affect people
who work in calendar cycles, and the accounting scale charts will
show peak activity as it relates to the official company calendar. Once
the graphs have been prepared, it is a simple matter to extrapolate,
and, therefore, predict how those indicators are changing. Again, the
actual numbers are not significant or even interesting and will never
impress the board of directors, but graphs that clearly show the trends
and general direction of user demands will be very useful.

A second useful measure is the total number of transactions
processed during a day or week for each application system. Both on-

line and batch applications usually have total counts which summarize the transaction and update activity in a specific production run or cycle. With only a little manual record keeping, it is easy to plot the trends of transactions by individual application systems and total installation. Such a graph is an accurate predictor of future increases or decreases in data center activity.

Another frequently overlooked measure of performance is the number of restarts with batch production jobs. Any production problem that causes a restart should be logged and tracked as a measure of both data center and application systems reliability. An increase in the number of restarts may indicate problems in the hardware, software, or application systems which should be investigated by management. Restarts by their very nature are a significant interruption in the normal job flow for both batch and on-line systems and can contribute to user dissatisfaction and decreased operational efficiency. The number of restarts, as well as their lost time, should be logged because there is a major qualitative difference between a restart that causes five minutes of lost time and one that costs two hours of processing activity.

In tracking restarts, it is essential to avoid placing blame or fault on the individuals or sections allegedly responsible for causing the interruption. Too often a restart tracking project will lead to hard feelings and frustrated employees because management looks upon the data collected as an easy way to place blame. If the management team follows the principle of "egoless management," however, these types of measurements will not cause ill feelings and disgruntled employees when they are used to help calmly and rationally resolve the causes of unnecessary production problems.

Reruns are even more valuable to help track data center performance, as long as the measuring procedure records the amount of time lost and the suspected cause. Again, an "egoless management" philosophy is the most effective management approach to follow when using actual statistics to discover the causes of specific operational problems. Blame should not be levied irresponsibly. Human egos can be very fragile.

For example, an increase in rerun activity can be due to several factors which may have little to do with the current staff or even the application systems. Even users can indirectly cause reruns by using incorrect instructions or invalid data. The processing load itself may increase so much in a short time that the operational staff cannot give production control proper attention. A high turnover in the operational staff will usually result in loss of valuable experience, which in turn leads to more errors and rerun problems. It is not a matter of fault or blame, but simply a matter of discovering specific reasons for an increase or even a decrease in rerun activity and acting accordingly. When a key staff member in the data center takes a vacation, it is not unusual to find that both reruns and restart activity will temporarily increase. Again, it is important to plot the trend of reruns and restarts rather than concentrate upon specific problems. A single error, mistake, or batch of bad data is interesting from a dramatic point of view, but the true management emphasis should be on the more significant long-term trends—not as dramatic, perhaps, but management concerns do not always have to be flashy.

Paper usage is an indicator which some installations find useful, especially if they have large printing volumes or require fast turnaround on printed reports. The trend toward more on-line updating and inquiry has reduced the need for printed reports in many computer centers and has fostered a policy of "exception reporting." Other large installations which still require hard-copy reports have gone to computer output microfilm (COM) as a means of reducing printed output. Some shops, however, still rely largely on the printed report, and a chart of paper usage is a good indicator of an increasing or decreasing workload.

The number of tapes in the tape library can also indicate trends for application systems which are tape oriented. A change in system architecture, such as a conversion from a tape-oriented system to mass storage or disk, will obviously negate such a measure. But for many organizations the total number of tapes plotted over a monthly basis is a good way to demonstrate increasing or decreasing tape usage.

Whatever indicators are selected to measure and track data center performance, management must ensure that the project is continuous. The responsibility for such measurement should be delegated to one person who understands its importance and who has both the time and resources necessary to gather and organize the data. Senior managers should also periodically reexamine their choice of measurements. The fact that a data center has used certain indicators for the past few years is no reason to always use those measures; perhaps a little research work and ingenuity can uncover better or more accurate indicators of data center performance.

CAPACITY PLANNING

Capacity planning is usually defined as the science of planning the hardware and software requirements of the future. Capacity planning has sometimes been compared to fortune telling and playing the horses. Managers charged with the responsibility for capacity planning and hardware purchasing usually take a deep breath, grab a rabbit's foot, scrounge around in vain for useful facts, and finally write their recommendations. However, with a few simple techniques the entire capacity planning process can be less terrifying and may even become reasonably accurate.

A program of periodic performance measurement will give the management team a set of charts and projections which will indicate the trend and direction of the changing production workload. Charts and graphs covering periods over one year will often show cyclical production peaks dependent on outside factors and, therefore, not indicative of capacity problems. For example, a retail company may experience its heaviest volume during the months before the Christmas season, but a normal temporary overload during that period should not by itself be an indication of a trend. Temporary capacity problems should be recognized for what they are.

Business data processing installations are often faced with continual changes in processing requirements. Only a few companies have a stable operating environment which allows performance analysts to ignore the possibility of changes. But time after time many data processing managers are surprised by capacity problems and poor performance caused by a new application system that appeared overnight, a sudden increase in the usage of a current system, or by a major user who has suddenly discovered all the potential features of an old application. Surprise is indeed a major cause of sudden capacity problems.

The only solution to this complex problem is to open the lines of communication among the data center operations management, the applications systems development management, and the user managers. The information necessary to adequately plan for future changes is available within the company, but gathering such information requires almost a constant effort from the DP management team. Without such information about future plans and activities, any manager attempting to plan future hardware capacity might as well roll a pair of dice.

Informal communication between others in the organization can be developed through a combination of interest and effort. That is, the operations management team should make a special effort to talk with users and applications systems management personnel on a regular but informal basis. Such contacts can be in the company cafeteria, in the hallway, or even in the restrooms. It is important for the DP staff to show a sincere interest in the activities of the user groups and in other sections of the MIS division. It is not a matter of spying or being nosy, but rather a matter of asking important questions when appropriate and listening when appropriate. The best and most useful information in the organization can sometimes be obtained simply by casual conversation!

Formal meetings between operational and user management are almost a requirement. A data processing management team who has contact with user groups only when specific problems or complaints arise is missing a chance to gain information that will not only help data processing discover problems before they become critical, but also will help significantly in capacity planning. User managers should be encouraged to share their formal and informal plans for expansion or modification of their current systems. It may take several repetitions, but the operational management team should stress that users must keep them posted on plans that might affect the hardware and software capabilities of the installation.

Another focus of capacity planning is to evaluate hardware and software configurations for specific applications in the data center. Of all the methods which can be used to compare CPUs and peripherals, one of the best is still the actual system test on the proposed hardware configurations. That is, techniques such as simulations or comparisons of such features as internal cycle speed of MIPS (millions of instructions per second) are valuable and should be used when possible, but the most effective means to evaluate potential hardware choices is to run the current software and application system on the new computer. Unfortunately, this is rarely possible, since it depends on the cooperation of the vendor and a current user in the same geo-graphical area. In other cases, the operating system software may be totally incompatible and a parallel test impossible.

The next choice is for the management team doing the hardware or software planning to contact users of the hardware in question and ask them to comment on the volume or capacity problems of the hardware. The number of transactions processed, the hours of operation of the data center, and the reliability of the hardware are all important topics that should be discussed.

Correct hardware management is a complex and difficult subject, in part because some experts concentrate exclusively on the technical aspects and thereby fail to bridge the gap between technical reports and management information. In a sense, the entire capacity-planning concept is an ideal candidate for the procedures and policies that have been espoused by the data processing profession for years. DP managers have told others in the company to use the computer to perform the detailed analyses but still apply the "human touch" to formulate the conclusions and recommendations which make sense to the people making the decisions. It is time for the data processing management team to follow its own advice.

Appendix

A

List of References

Successful data processing management is a never-ending battle, and a large part of that battle is the continuous education and reeducation required to keep up with the hardware, software, and people being managed. Just as technology does not stand still, neither does advancement in the management sciences or in the technical data processing aspects of management. Also, people themselves grow and develop over the years, and what is right for a manager at one career stage may not be right at another. Organizational structures and philosophies often require new approaches or management techniques. The best way to survive in this ever-changing environment is for managers to continually read source materials and consider new theories, developments, and practices. They may not agree with any specific individual theory, but they must learn that management style can always improve.

The reference books listed here are only a sampling of the available resource material for data processing managers who wish to broaden their horizons and embark upon a continuous program of self-education.

American Bar Association. *Computers and the Law—An Introductory Handbook.* Chicago: Commerce Clearing House, 1981.

American Management Institute. *How to Manage a Data Processing Department.* New York: AMA Extension Institute, 1981.

Bennett, Roger. *Managing Personnel and Performance.* New York: Wiley, 1981.

Bostwick, Burdette E. *3 Proven Techniques and Strategies for Getting the Job Interview.* New York: Wiley, 1981.

Cummings, Paul W. *Open Management.* New York: Amacom, 1980.

French, Jack. *Up the DP Pyramid.* New York: Wiley, 1981.

Holdz, Herman and Terry Schmidt. *The Winning Proposal.* New York: McGraw-Hill, 1981.

Hughes, Charles L. *Goal Setting.* New York: Amacom, 1965.

Imundo, Louis V. *The Effective Supervisors Handbook.* New York: Amacom, 1980.

Juran, J. M. *Managerial Breakthrough.* New York: McGraw-Hill, 1981.

Karling, Marvin. *The Human Use of Human Resources.* New York: McGraw-Hill, 1981.

Keen, Jeffery S. *Managing Systems Development.* New York: Wiley, 1981.

Koontz, Harold, and Cyril O'Donnel. *Essentials of Management,* second edition. New York: McGraw-Hill, 1968.

Long, Larry E. *Data Processing Documentation and Procedures Manual.* Reston, Virginia: Reston, 1980.

Mali, Paul. *Managing by Objectives.* New York: Wiley, 1972.

Martin, James. *Application Development Without Programmers.* Englewood Cliffs, N.J.: Prentice-Hall, 1981.

Mason, Joseph. *How to Build Your Management Skills.* New York: McGraw-Hill, 1965.

McCay, James. *The Management of Time.* Englewood Cliffs, N.J.: Prentice-Hall, 1959.

McCosh, A. M., M. Rahman, and M. J. Earl. *Developing Managerial Information Systems.* New York: Wiley, 1981.

Odiorne, George. *How Managers Make Things Happen.* Englewood Cliffs, N.J.: Prentice-Hall, 1961.

Rullo, Thomas A., Ed. *Advances in Computer Programming Management.* Rochelle Park, N. J.: Hayden, 1981.

Schaeffer, Howard. *Data Center Operations.* Englewood Cliffs, N.J.: Prentice-Hall, 1981.

Siu, R. G. *The Master Manager.* New York: Wiley, 1981.

Strauss, Melvin J. *Computer Capacity.* New York: Van Nostrand Reinhold, 1981.

Strauss, G. and L. Sayles. *Personnel–The Human Problems of Management*, 4th ed. Englewood Cliffs, N.J.: Prentice-Hall, 1980.

Talbot, J. R. *Management Guide to Computer Security.* New York: Wiley, 1981.

Walsh, Myles. *Understanding Computers: What Managers and Users Need to Know.* New York: Wiley, 1981.

B

The Management
Plan of Action

To develop good managers, a company or organization needs a specific plan of action to accomplish that goal. The following steps can be used in a long-term program to train and expand the management skills of junior, middle, and even senior data processing executives. Following this plan will not be easy, but the final results will be worth the price.

1.   Admit that your organization has a problem with data processing managers. Even the most accomplished and successful management team can still learn valuable techniques to improve its performance and the total performance of its individual sections. Managing a data processing organization is a complex combination of science, art, skill, and black magic. A continual training and educa-

tional program for managers can improve the science, art, and skill aspects, and three out of four is a pretty good average anytime.

2.   Weed out the managers who refuse to admit they can learn from a management training program, or who firmly believe they are "perfect" managers. Unless by some miracle (or knowledge of magic) they truly are "perfect" managers, those individuals will be a long-term drain on the entire department. They will be like lumbering, ponderous dinosaurs trying to survive in a world where the rules concerning software, hardware, and people are changing every year.

3.   Very slowly begin to weed out the managers at every level who were forced into management positions because they were senior technicians and who have no real desire to remain managers. Many highly qualified professionals can make substantial contributions to their organizations by staying in the technical ranks, and a salary structure that forces them to remain managers merely to receive appropriate salary increases is self-destructive. The only thing worse than a manager who thinks he or she is automatically an expert at management is one who has no desire to function as a manager and would rather be a well-paid technician.

4.   Appoint one person in the organization to be the management trainer, who will function as the coordinator for the entire project. This individual could be a senior executive, a personnel department employee, or even a new data processing manager who is honest enough to admit that he or she needs help in meeting responsibilities.

5.   Require every supervisor and manager to fill out an "Attitude Evaluation Checklist" (see Appendix C). Each individual should be told to go through the checklist slowly, carefully, and privately. Senior management may require people to answer the questions in writing. The answers and opinions should be treated as confidential information to be used only in a project to improve management performance and *not* as an evaluation tool for the individual manager. That is, supervisors who think that their written responses will determine their next performance rating or salary increase may not answer the questions honestly, and this task will be a waste of time for all concerned. Conversely, if senior management cannot guarantee the confidentiality of these answers, the managers should not turn in any written responses. A practical alternative is to let the personnel director or "management trainer" keep all written responses.

6.   The person responsible for the training project should hold a

group meeting to discuss the checklist and the implications of the responses. People should never be forced to reveal their own answers, but rather, encouraged to share their attitudes and feelings about management in general. If time is a problem and people complain about their heavy workload, a luncheon meeting is the ideal answer The company should provide the meal. At least two hours of honest discussion are required if the participants are to learn anything from a group encounter.

7.   With the assistance of the management group (and the experienced senior technical staff), develop a written list of the most serious problems in the data processing organization. Identify them in detail and be careful not to place blame on any individual or section. Constantly emphasize the point that problems affect everyone, are the responsibility of the entire organization, and can ultimately be solved with proper planning and commitment. Look for those long-range problems that rear their ugly heads time and time again, and for those underlying problems that are hard to pinpoint but tend to undermine the hard work of the data processing department. Lack of training, for example, may be one underlying problem.

8.   Distribute the list to the entire staff. Don't worry about the possible demoralizing effect on the employees—they already know the major problems even if they have never verbalized or listed them! If new employees are not aware of such problem areas they will be soon enough. Rather, discuss the situation in a calm, professional, and positive manner. Managers at every level must reveal that they recognize deficiencies and are willing to face them as a challenge. For example, one statement could be, "If the lack of communication between programming and operations is causing all sorts of misunderstandings, reruns, and production problems, then aren't we smart enough to develop ways to solve that problem?" The emphasis should be upon solving problems, not allocating blame.

9.   Set priorities for the items of the problem list, not only in terms of their seriousness but with some indication of how easily each problem can be solved. That is, a highly visible problem that occupies number six on a list could be made number one if the solution is easy. Showing immediate and positive results will help boost morale.

10.   Using the resources in this book, develop a management training program which will run concurrently with the specific proj-

ects to solve problems in the data processing organization. Many serious problems *cannot* be solved unless senior executives realize that managers must themselves improve their approaches and attitudes toward their employees and their positions. Managers and supervisors should meet regularly to discuss general management-level issues, as opposed to specific problem areas. Topics for discussion could include such issues as handling difficult employees, quality control, or meeting user imposed deadlines with limited resources. Specific problem areas should be postponed for another meeting. Managers at all levels can learn a great deal from each other, and they should periodically review their own performances and management style. Managers may not be satisfied with what they see, but self-examination is a necessary activity.

11.   Develop solutions to each problem according to its priority. Never go overboard and ask for impossible or costly answers which cannot be implemented. If a specific problem cannot be solved, admit it and focus on problems that can. Use the chapters in this book, reference materials, and discussions with other managers, groups, and employees. It is amazing how much managers can learn when they shut their mouths and open their ears.

12.   Go back to step one. The second and third time around should be easier, but the job of moving data processing management out of the Dark Ages will be a continuous battle. With the right attitude and determination, it could even be fun.

C

Attitude Evaluation Checklist

Answer all questions honestly and be prepared to give reasons for each of your answers.

1   How many times a week do you use the word "boss"? Do you over use it? Do other managers use that term as much as you do?

2   When you talk to your employees, do you casually mention the fact that you are their manager?

3   Do you ever tell employees it is their main responsibility to satisfy you? Is that what you really want from subordinates?

4   Do you always give credit to specific employees when discussing accomplishments with your own manager?

5   When an employee makes a mistake, do you invariably mention his or her name to your manager?

6   Do you go out of your way to consistently share information about company goals and plans with your own staff?

7   Do you give staff members or subordinate managers a clear understanding of the purpose behind each assignment or project?

8   Do you hold regularly scheduled conferences at least once a week with each person who reports to you?

9   When a project is completed successfully, do you allow the staff involved to "spread the good news," or do you reserve that announcement for yourself?

10   If you are a second- or third-level manager, do you regularly speak to employees two or more levels below you in the hierarchy?

11   Without consulting records, can you discuss in detail the following topics for each of your employees?

Age
Education
Living status (home or apartment, section or area)
Family status (married, children, etc.)
Where he or she spent the last vacation
Employment history
What activities he or she likes and does not like in the job
Technical or managerial strengths and weaknesses
Favorite leisure time activities

12   When was the last time you had lunch with your entire staff?

13   Do you know what projects or activities each employee completed during the past year, and how each individual felt about those projects?

14   For each person who reports to you, list the most frustrating job-related responsibility he or she faces according to his or her own perception.

15   How often do you sit down with each employee and discuss career goals as they relate to the organization? Do you know in detail the professional goals of each person who reports to you?

16   Do you have another manager in your office in whom you can confide and discuss job-related matters?

17   How would you feel about hiring an employee who would earn more than you?

18   How often do you formally review employees? Do you follow the company guidelines? Are you satisfied with them?

19   How often do you accept an employee's suggestion? Are you afraid to upset the status quo? Do you discuss every proposed change with your own manager before coming to a decision?

20 Do your employees or subordinate managers frequently come to you with suggestions?

21 How often do you "explode" in anger or use foul and abusive language when talking to employees?

22 Do you let personal feelings, such as a prejudice against minorities, affect your hiring or salary recommendations?

23 Do you normally "fight for your people?" Is that a wise idea in your company?

24 Do your employees treat you with respect?

25 Do other sections treat your employees with respect?

Index